THE ART OF SURFCASTING WITH LURES

ZENO HROMIN

All inquiries should be address to
Zeno Hromin, P.O. Box 10665
Westbury, N.Y. 11590
or visit our website at
www.zenohromin.com

Fourth Printing

IBSN 978-1-60461-478-7

Design and Layout: Stacey Kruk

Cover Design: Alberto Knie

Illustrations and Artwork: Tommy Corrigan

— DEDICATION —

I would like to dedicate this book to my grandfather Vinko, who always had time to take me fishing. Although he is not with us any more I know he still is watching over me.

To my wife who puts up with my frequent excursions and yet still somehow finds time to sit and listen to me describe my trips in excruciating detail. I am humbled by your understanding and kindness. Your unconditional love and support is the main reason why this book project has become a reality.

To Steven, my son and my fishing partner, I offer thanks for your companionship and unbridled enthusiasm any time a rod is in your hands.

To my daughter Michelle, whose smile can light up a room, I offer thanks for your unwavering support. Seeing your smile after a long night in the surf makes my life even more beautiful.

— ACKNOWLEDGMENTS —

It is kind of ironic that the words that I might consider most important in this book might be the ones that will be read the least. Most readers will merely glance through the acknowledgments before moving to the rest of the book. However, I urge you to stick around for a moment because without these generous and incredibly talented people this book would only exist as a figment of my imagination.

To my dear friends, Edward J. Messina and Roger Martin, I offer eternal gratitude. They have labored mightily editing my writing, trying to remove all the "Zenoisms" out of each chapter. Without their editing skills, this book would never have seen the light of day.

A great deal of appreciation goes to my dear friend Tommy Corrigan who skillfully designed all the artwork in these pages. His youthful exuberance and his passion for surfcasting are infectious and have often inspired me to do things that I thought I was not capable of doing.

To all the members of High Hill Striper Club, past and present, I offer my gratitude for your guidance and support over the years. Without your advice and support I would have never written this book. Without your friendships I don't want to imagine what my life would be.

Special thanks goes to Fred Golofaro, Senior editor of The Fisherman magazine and Gene Bourque, former editor of On the Water magazine for their support and encouragement over the years. Both of these fine gentlemen always found the time to answer my questions and guide me in the right direction in all matters including my writings. You truly are "two of a kind."

Appreciation also goes to one of the most skillful and incredibly talented surfcasters on the east coast, "Crazy" Alberto Knie for his advice, honest critique and guidance.

To the people who helped with advice regarding this project I offer my sincerest thanks. My close friend Robert Maina, Joe Lyons from

Surfcasting-rhodeisland.com and Peter Graeber from Saltwateredge.com, they have often served as sounding boards and offered honest and unbiased suggestions and advice during the process of writing this book.

Special thanks goes to Bill "Doc" Muller, one of the east coast's most recognized surfcasters and a prolific outdoor writers. His articles in The Fisherman and his books have inspired thousands to join the ranks of the surf fishing community, including yours truly.

I also want to express my sincerest appreciation to all my friends who let me use their pictures in this book. Their generosity and support of this project means more to me than I can ever express in words. Thanks to Adam Flax, John Skinner, Mark DeAngelis, Manny Moreno, Peter Graeber, Gasper Lapiana, Mike Wright, Peter Jordan, Al Albano, Nick Colabro, Peter Hewlett, Peter Peresh, James Sylvester, Bill Wetzel, Toby Lipinski, Steve McKenna, Saltwater Edge in Newport,RI, "Iron"Mike Everin, Vito Orlando, Garry Moore, Scott Cunningham, Dominic Morandi, Lenny Ferro, Robert Maina, "Crazy" Alberto Knie, Freddie's Bait and Tackle in Montauk, Chris Wahl, Terence Kirby, David Ryng, Tom Alterson, Dennis O'Connell, David Mangone, Carol Ann Tobias, Josh Clogston, Shark River Surf Anglers and Michael Ludlow.

— Zeno Hromin

— FOREWORD —

Having offered me the privilege of introducing the reader to this book, I find that the information contained in it has been long overdue. It sets a precedent with regard to fishing with lures providing instruction on Where, When, Why and most importantly HOW! Nuances usually overlooked by novices and seasoned anglers are covered such as selection for proper conditions, seasons and bait imitation. The book is loaded with key ideas which mark Zeno's distinctive contribution to the world of saltwater plug fishing.

One of the remarkable things about Zeno Hromin is that he has used his imagination, pragmatic judgments, immense energy and humor to develop a book explaining all aspects of surf fishing with plugs. He wants to share his knowledge based on years of experience in the surf and he achieves his goal! Surf fishing is an art, hence the title of this book. If you absorb the lessons in this book you will master the art of using the many fine lures available to the fisherman today.

He shares his childhood days as a hand-lining gaff boy fishing with his grandfather in Croatia. He describes his first day of surf fishing when he ventured barefoot onto a slippery south shore jetty and discovered the dangers of tide and waves. Yet, in spite of these rude awakenings, he lives to tell the story. Through his passion and dedication to this sport, he prepares the reader to become a better fisherman by reaching into his own bag of tricks and coming up with the techniques best-suited to the conditions we encounter while fishing. He instills in us the confidence to develop our own angling strategies.

From the essential tools of the trade, smart strategies and worthy tips, Zeno shares it all cleverly and with great, humbling wit. The underlying theme of this book is the secret to becoming a better fisherman with lures... and I highly and strongly recommend it!

Tight Lines,

"Crazy" Alberto Knie

— TABLE OF CONTENTS —

— INTRODUCTION —

Have you ever fished next to a surfcaster who was hooking up on every cast while you drew blanks? I certainly have on many occasions. Do you think that his success was a result of his gear being superior to yours? Probably not. Most likely the reason for his prowess was his ability to present his lure to the structure he was targeting in such a way that the gamefish found it too irresistible to pass up. Over the years I found out that my casting distance, brand of lure or even the color the lure, has very little to do with my success. I used to tear my shoulder apart trying to be the one who cast the furthest. I bought lures that were in such high demand I could have bought dozens of others instead of overpaying for the latest "hot" lure. Fortunately for my sanity and my wallet, I realized that there is no such thing as "a must have lure." I also found out that my success was dependent on the careful placement and retrieval of my lure while taking into consideration the effects of wind, moon, current and tide on the structure I was targeting. My casts over the years have become shorter but more intense as I gained knowledge and the confidence that comes with that knowledge.

Today, I am as comfortable with placing a metal lip swimmer on the backside of a folding wave only twenty yards away as I am in launching a pencil popper over the distant sandbar. Figuring out which lure would give us the best chance of enticing a fish to strike is, in my opinion, the surfcaster's ultimate challenge. Tossing a lure designed to work on the surface into deep water is about as effective as casting a darter into water without current. Today's surfcaster has more lures to chose from then any other generation before and although they all might catch fish at some time or another, each lure is designed to be most effective under specific conditions. Some lures excel in fast moving water, wobbling tantalizingly side to side while in slow water they show almost no action at all. Some are known for their ability to cut through the strongest wind like a hot knife through butter while others are tossed around in these same conditions like a feather. I wrote this book hoping to demystify the process of choosing which lures to use and how to work them in order to get the most out of the action they are designed to produce.

Of course, knowing which lure to use is only the beginning of our quest. Having the right lure, in the right place but under the wrong conditions is almost like having a pen in which the ink has dried. Yeah, it worked great once but not today! This is why the first half of the book is dedicated to gear, structure, the effects of wind, tide, moons and currents, baitfish profiles and strategies. These are all things that must be taken into consideration before the lure is even selected. The chapter on confidence might not seem that important at first glance but I assure you that following the advice in that chapter will put more fish on the beach for you than any other chapter in this book. The second half of the book is dedicated to individual profiles of the most popular lures used in the surf today. This section contains an in-depth analysis of what, where and why to use each lure coupled with a discussion on colors and sizes that are most productive. This should go a long way toward answering any questions you might have about the most popular plugs on the market today. There is also a tip at the end of each lure chapter which should help you turn your ordinary lure into an extraordinary one under certain conditions.

What you won't find in this book is a discussion on fishing with live or dead bait. The effectiveness of tossing live, rigged or dead bait is undeniable, particularly when it comes to targeting large fish. I am certainly not one who sticks his nose up in the air and looks down on those who do it regularly. There is an art to baitfishing too but fishing with lures remains my passion. While plugging, learn about structure, wave formation, weather patterns and tides and you can apply this knowledge quite successfully to fishing with bait as I've done on many occasions.

The thought of standing in the surf while getting rocked by waves, all while my drag is singing under the strain of a good fish is enough to send shivers down my spine. I am a Plug-a-holic, not a sharpie, celebrity or a great fisherman. I am just a surfcaster who often finds success through sheer perseverance and determination. Most of all I consider myself very fortunate to have friends who over the years selflessly shared their knowledge with me. This book is in part a result of their generosity because it would probably take me a few lifetimes to learn all the strategies and techniques on my own.

You might question just what is the "art" in surf fishing with lures? I assure you it's there. Just like an artist uses his brush to create a masterpiece on a canvas, a surfcaster does the same thing except the vast ocean waters serve as his canvas. He paints his own picture with a metal lip that he is working at proper speed so it's quivering in the white foam behind a rushing wave. He might also be using his rod like a magic wand, working a pencil popper or breathing life into a bucktail in the deep inlet rip with a slight flick of a wrist. Just like an artist who carefully lays out his color pallet before ever making a single stroke on canvas, a surfcaster carefully plans each trip, taking into consideration wind, tide, moon period, current, water conditions, availability of bait and structure he might be targeting. After all this preparation, the actual strike of a fish taking the lure serves only to validate our approach.

Toward the end of the book you will find chapters on conservation and fishing with kids, two things that are very dear to me. I think you'll agree that we must do our part to protect this valuable resource so that our children can enjoy surf casting the beaches as much as we do.

CHAPTER ONE

— MEMORIES OF A FIRST LURE —

I'll never forget the first plugs I ever bought. I was just getting started in the sport of surfcasting and I turned for advice to a trusted friend. He had an affinity for plastic plugs; Bombers in particular were his favorites and that's what he recommended. I remember sitting in an apartment in New York City and browsing through the Bass Pro magazine, excited like a kid on Christmas Eve yet totally confused by the array of lures, styles and colors. The fact that I had no clue what to do with these plugs or how to use them didn't deter me from purchasing them.

This was in the 1980's and I had just arrived in New York on a plane from Croatia without the benefit of knowing a single word of English or ever seeing a fishing rod or reel in my life. All my fishing to this point was done in Europe via hand lining. We used a piece of heavy Styrofoam to serve as a tool for winding a line and for a "drag" we used our fingers. When you had a big fish on you applied the "drag" by squeezing your line between your thumb and index finger. Needless to say this was a very painful exercise, as even the thick mono would cut the index finger to the bone under pressure of a large red snapper or a small tuna. I am afraid to think about what would have happened had we used braided line in those days. I might not even have a finger to type and write this book. It may seem strange but as I grew older my hands became so hard and leathery that by the time I reached my teenage years they resembled those of my beloved grandfather even though there was more than a fifty year difference in our ages.

It was my grandfather, along with my grandmother, who took care of me after my parents divorced while I was just a kid. I can remember as if it were yesterday the trips my Grandpa and I made in our 21-foot wooden boat powered by a 7 horsepower wind-on German car engine. It was a loud beast, slow on speed but dependable and easily maintained. My grandfather was a boat mechanic by trade and he worked on boats in my village on the Adriatic coast to supplement his meager pension. He did that and he fished any chance he got. He was considered a master fisherman in those days, finding shoals in the middle of nowhere and setting up on fish with the use of only land markings while others drifted around him without a clue. The only electronics we had were two running lights and even those were sparingly used so as not to drain the car battery stowed in the cabin.

We would get up at 3 A.M., head out to the sea and set the long lines by hand. Once the lines were set we would then go hand lining for a few hours until it was time to pick up the long lines we had laid out in the morning. The rest of the day was spent standing on the bow and hand lining for red snappers till dusk when it would be time to head back to the port closest to the fishing grounds. There was no winch so my grandfather pulled all the long lines over his shoulder while I served as the gaff man. Since this wasn't a pleasure cruise and every fish counted as income I was often on the receiving end of stares or some piercing looks if I would miss a fish while gaffing. My grandfather preferred uninhabited islands to make a camp and we would throw an anchor in the small harbor while he would make a dinner. After we fished all day my hands reeked of the sardines and squid that we used for bait and this is something I accepted as a part of my every day life. But when he made dinner and I started getting a whiff of what was in the pot I had to hold my gag reflex in check. Now my grandfather was also considered one of the best cooks around and people came from miles away to our humble home and begged him to cater meals for their gatherings but on these trips, after staring at fish all day the last thing I wanted see in the pot was......fish! If it was quality stuff like a striper or sea bass but no, those were marked for sale. I had the pleasure of feasting on bergals, sand porgies and sand sharks. After dinner we would attach bait to the long lines for the morning drop and then he would have a bit of home made red wine and we would crawl into the cabin to sleep. This went on for three or four days or as long as it took to fill the homemade freezers we had on board.

The good thing was that upon the return we were spared going to the fish market. Since he had a great reputation as the top fisherman in the area his entire catch was pre-sold and restaurateurs came to our house to pick out the best fish. The smaller stuff went to our neighbors in the village while we got bergals and of course, sand sharks. Once in a while I'd be pleasantly surprised to smell, through out the house, the aroma of large skate wings in garlic stew. Even though we lacked many of the things I consider today to be necessities, the love that my grandparents gave me more than made up for them and I never really felt I was missing out on anything. My grandfather passed away a few years ago but the love of fishing he instilled in me will be with me forever.

Anyway, enough of my digression, let's get back to those plastic Bombers from the Bass Pro catalog. One day they arrive along with my first rod and reel. It was a Penn reel and a 10-foot rod that had as much action as a long broomstick. Since I was a teenager and soaked up English like a sponge it didn't take long for me to start browsing through the pages of the Long Island Fisherman magazine. For the most part I had no clue what they were talking about when they were describing "rips" or "sand bars" but I knew enough to decipher where good catches were taking place by reading the report section.

One day after reading of good action on a jetty at Jones Beach State Park, I packed my gear in my car and headed in that direction. After a two mile walk through the soft sand I finally reached the jetty but immediately understood just how unprepared I was for what was about to take place. In Croatia I fished barefoot and that's how I reached the jetty but one look at the anglers on the jetty told me either I was out of my mind or the guys on it were overdressed. All the anglers were dressed in gear I had never seen as they had waders, creepers and jackets. All of them except a single guy at the tip who was in shorts and sneakers. I figured since he made it out there I could too. This jetty was rebuilt in recent years but in those days it had a few large holes and openings where you had to time

Sights like these are one of the reasons I fell in love with the surf.

the waves which were crashing through these holes and then quickly make a dash across before getting swept away. Needless to say, there I was in the middle of this gaping hole in the jetty, standing barefoot on a slimy rock and looking at this mountain of water coming in my direction, praying to God I get out alive. The wave slammed me into the rocks and my legs gave way from under me and my back slammed into a boulder. I held onto the last boulder with all my might as another few inches and I was going to be washed off into the inlet. Somehow I managed to crawl into the hole in between two rocks before the next wave rushed over me then I quickly stood up and made a dash out of the quagmire. By the time I reached the tip of the jetty my shins were bleeding, my back was bruised but I was undeterred. I was going to catch fish, come hell or high water. Well, it was high water that did me in. Only after I got onto the tip of the jetty and looked back did I realize that the water was coming up and filling the hole through which I had just climbed. Panicked and confused I was consoled by the friendly surfcaster, who told me that the tide would recede in a few hours but not before he justly scolded me for showing up on the jetty barefoot.

Now I am standing at the tip of the jetty armed with all the information I had read with regard to which knots to tie, the length of the leader and even how to cast, or at least I thought so. I opened the bail, leaned into the rod that barely bent and made a cast. A loud pop filled the air like a shot from a rifle. Not knowing what happened, I reeled until all the line came back through the guides and started spinning on the spool. Realizing my lure was gone I looked around in embarrassment as I proceeded to re-tie a rig. As I opened my K-Mart special surf bag and pulled out another Bomber, I did not realize that its trebles would catch those of the other plugs and so they all came out of the bag at once. Trying to shake them off and to get them out of my bag I managed to drop three in the abyss between the jetty boulders, never to be seen again. Now I was down to two plugs. On the next cast, I immediately snapped off the next to last Bomber and watched in horror as it went sailing into the sea. Now I found myself paralyzed by fear, down to my last plug and not a single one back in my car. Even if I did have one, how was I going to get there? I was not going to walk two miles in each direction to get them on bleeding limbs. Besides, I had to wait for the tide to drop in order to get back. So I tied on my last Bomber and made as soft a cast as possible knowing full well I was

Rocky beaches and jetties are favorite hunting grounds of striped bass.

moments away from having no plugs.

At this point I didn't really care about catching fish but was more intent on working on my casting technique so that I would not lose plugs in the future. As I reeled the plug to the base of the jetty, it got "stuck" on the rocks, or so I thought. Imagine my surprise when the "rock" started to move and thrashed wildly at the base of the jetty. A decent striper was attached to the Bomber and was going absolutely berserk. Nobody told me about the need to adjust the drag and since I was unfamiliar with its purpose I tightened it to the max. The strength of the striper and the barnacle encrusted rocks did their thing and the line soon parted above the leader. Now you might think losing all your plugs, standing stranded on the jetty bruised and defeated would make a person reconsider his actions and the thought of fishing again, but that wasn't the case. My desire to become proficient at surfcasting only increased as a result of that disastrous trip. After all, I just hooked my first fish and you know what? I think I was hooked more than the fish and remain so to this day!

CHAPTER TWO

— GEAR —

In the old days surfcasters have been looked upon as anglers who couldn't afford a boat. Frankly, I don't think this was true then any more than it is now. There is something special about watching those first rays of sun rise above the eastern sky while casting your lure in the crest of the wave, knowing that your next cast might be the one that produces that fish of a lifetime. Or standing perched on a rock in the stillness of the night with only your drag breaking the silence. I have yet to meet a surf fisherman who would rather go fishing on his boat than stand waist deep in the surf, getting buffeted by waves. As far as the notion that surfcasters can't afford a boat, darned if I don't know dozens of surf anglers who carry more gear in their trucks than many boats are worth. So much for surfcasters being cheapskates! Boat anglers have the luxury of fishing in a somewhat protected environment and have at their disposal every lure or tool they can possible carry with them on board. The surfcaster needs to have gear on him to keep him dry and comfortable. He needs a light to guide his way, a bag to carry his lures, a belt to keep the water out of his waders and a large scale to weigh in the monster he is about to catch.

Fortunately, today's surfcaster has a bigger selection to choose from than any generation of anglers before him. Before the surfcaster can enjoy catching fish he must comfortable. If you are wet, cold or the wind is sending shivers down your spine, I can almost guarantee you are not going to enjoy yourself. Let's take a look at some basic equipment every surfcaster should have and some not so basic items that in my view are indispensable.

WADERS

Waders might be the single most important part of a surfcaster's gear, yet many anglers concentrate strictly on price instead of the quality of the item. When choosing a pair of waders, I would suggest that you forgo buying cheap rubber ones as they will make you sweat profusely during

Even in calmer waters waders are necessary in order to stay warm and dry.

most of the season. On the other end of the spectrum, waders that cost hundreds of dollars have so far proven to be very disappointing for saltwater anglers. Most of these models were designed for freshwater anglers and little thought was given to the fact that we constantly hold our long rods between our legs resulting in worn out stitching and leaks at the crotch seams. Mid priced models, preferably from manufacturers that cater to saltwater anglers and made out of breathable material, should provide you with lasting comfort and consequently add to your surfcasting experience. Double taped seams and some reinforcement at the knees and behind are preferable, especially if you are planning to climb over barnacle covered rocks and boulders.

A few years ago I waded onto a rock at Montauk Point on the south side with my friend Peter. To get to this very large boulder, we had to wade through water about chest high, but it was worth it as the rock was large enough for both of us to fish on it comfortably. We caught nothing that day but we did have lots of laughs and after a few hours we decided to head back to town. I slid off the rock on my behind only to feel barnacles ripping through my waders and water gushing in through the hole. By the time I reached dry land my waders were filled with water and to add insult to the misery, I was facing an hour long walk back to my buggy. I laugh about it today, but it sure wasn't funny at the time.

Although I wear size 12 shoes, I usually opt for a size 13 boot on the waders. This allows for extra room in the boot so that I can put on an extra pair of comfy wool socks in cold weather. In addition, the extra socks provide for additional comfort, by absorbing the impact of the hard surfaces during long walks on rocks or boulders. I prefer my waders to be made of the lightest material possible instead of heavily insulated fabric. Following this strategy allows you to wear the waders during warm weather and cold weather and just about all year long. This saves money as you will not require a second set for extreme conditions. During the colder weather you can always add layers of light thin thermal clothes underneath. Today's lightweight waders weigh mere ounces without including the weight of the boots and have come a long ways in providing durability and comfort. Gone are the days when you took your waders off after a trip only to find your clothes drenched in sweat. Even better, some of the leading manufacturers today offer absolutely incredible warranties so you can buy their product without fear that it will not stand up to the harsh saltwater environment. If for some reason they do not, then all you have to do is send it back to the manufacturer and they will usually exchange them without any hassle.

Wader styles range from the hip boot length, to the chest high length with either a stocking or boot foot. In my opinion you should really only consider the boot foot models if you're planning to make them your primary pair of waders. The stocking foot can be more comfortable on rocky terrain as the separate shoe worn with these waders usually provides for a better fit and more support around the ankle than the boot foot wader. However, once you step on sandy beaches the stocking foot waders have a tendency to fill the up with sand, making walking extremely uncomfortable. Hip boots really have no place in the surf as the constant pounding of the ocean waves will soak you in no time, especially at the most critical moment when you are attempting to beach a fish.

Even wading on marshes in the back bays can prove to be an unpleasant experience with hip boots. When I was just getting started in the sport, I got a pair of hip boots from an old-timer who used them while fresh water fishing in upstate New York. One afternoon, I decided to fish the drains on the backside of Gilgo Beach on Long Island. I will never be able to purge the memory of this escapade from my mind. Looking from the road, the green marshes that lay in front of me extended from the road to the State Channel and appeared as green and unbroken as a football field. Only when I started wading on them did I realize that there were many drains and ditches that run within the marshes itself. Armed with my K-Mart rod and a bunch of small plastic Creek Chub lures, I grudgingly waded for almost an hour to the water line. Finally, after a tough walk I reached the water but not exactly where I wanted to be. Some of the drains and dips were too deep to cross in the hip boots so I had to settle for another spot. Once I got settled at the mouth of a large drain I started casting a little Creek Chub darter into the channel. Fortunately, or unfortunately, depending upon your point of view, I was soon to find out that this drain was loaded with schoolie stripers chasing spearing. I felt pretty good about myself at that moment. Concentrating intently on the presentation of my lure, I paid no attention to the rising water or the sunlight disappearing over the New York City skyline. Suddenly a black cloud engulfed me. It was thousands upon thousands of mosquitoes that must have risen from the swampy waters. I swear to you, they seemed so thick that you could cut through them with a knife. I had never experienced anything like that before so I started to panic. I had a long way to go, to get back to my truck, and I had no bug spray with me. Now I was starting to lose sight of the road in the gathering twilight and was getting disoriented. The little blood suckers were doing their best to zone in on any place where my skin was exposed. I could barely keep my eyes open and was sweating profusely when I decided to ditch the rod in the creek. I began to run alongside of the edge of the creek and make a break for the road. Now, you can probably imagine the extent of my panic at this point, as I was willing to give up my rod because it was slowing me down. Now I had another free hand to swat at the mosquitoes, as if that was going to help!

Running through the marshes at full speed, unencumbered by the rod, I had no idea there were other drainage channels that were not visible in the twilight until I stepped into one and sunk to my chest in soft mud. My hip boots were now filled with water and I was getting eaten alive by bugs. For a few seconds, I thought of ditching the boots too! However, the idea of running over the marshes barefoot was even worse than what I was experiencing at the time. Somehow I got myself back onto the marsh and realized I couldn't run with hip boots full of water. I lay down on the grass and put my feet in the air draining the mud and water from my boots. I fell a few more times, more then I care to remember! I was tripping on unseen logs and debris, falling into ditches along the way, while all this time the mosquitoes were mercilessly pecking at my face. By the time I got into my truck, my face was swollen like a watermelon, welts on top of welts, some the size of tangerines! Talk about a painful experience. I swore right then and there that hip boots would never, ever be worn over my tired, muddy and wet feet.

WETSUIT

If you are planning to spend a lot of time on jetties or in rocky areas investing in a wetsuit might be a smart proposition. Safety is always a concern when fishing in these often inhospitable places. Wearing a wetsuit goes a long way to addressing some of the issues that can crop up. If you get washed off the rocks or even worse a jetty, the wetsuit will help you as it is naturally buoyant and you can literally float in it to safety. The buoyancy of the wet suit will also make it easier to wade out to the rocks that are off limits to the wader wearing angler. Since you are already wet in your wetsuit you don't need to be concerned too much about getting knocked off a rock. As a result you can pay more attention to protecting yourself and your rod and reel. I personally find that wearing a wetsuit increases my comfort when fishing in rough water but I should mention that it also seems to increase the level of my stupidity as I often try to get on rocks that I would not even dream about if I was wearing waders. I find that the Farmer John style is much more versatile than a full body suit, as I can wear it in the summer with just a tee shirt under it. In the early fall I can wear a light jacket and later in the year a heavy neoprene jacket to keep

Wetsuit wearing anglers have an advantage when it comes to wading onto the far rocks or distant sandbars.

warm. When it comes to the thickness of the neoprene, 3.5 mm is pretty good for the warmer months while a 5 mm suit is ideal for early spring and fall. Some anglers wear 7 mm suits and others even suit up in a dry suit. However, I find either of these two options to be best utilized for the coldest months of the year. If you end up spending a lot of time in a wetsuit you will soon find out pretty fast that as with anything else in this sport, there is no "one size fits all" answer. I suggest you start with a 5 mm suit rather than a 3.5 mm suit. The lighter versions are great while you are getting dressed and wading out to the rocks in the summer, but I often get cold when I spend a considerable amount of time in the water, even in the summer. Regardless of how good the fishing might be on any given night, you won't enjoy the experience if you are shivering. If I had to choose one thickness and style it would be a 5mm Farmer John type wetsuit because of its versatility.

JACKETS

Those who are new to the sport generally forgo purchasing a jacket but they quickly find out that this seemingly unimportant item is indispensable when fishing in the suds. They figure the waders are keeping them dry and they already spent a good amount of money on a rod, reel and lures, the jacket is something they can live without. Besides, a new angler usually spends most of his time plugging in the daytime and most likely only under fair weather conditions. Then the fall run happens and they are pelted by freezing rain, buffeted by cold north winds and often greeted by angry, foaming seas. They quickly realize that a surf top is as indispensable as any other part of a surfcaster's gear. Fortunately, today's anglers have a myriad of styles and materials to choose from as well as a broad price range. Granted, on nice sunny days just about any jacket will keep you dry from splashes in the surf but you really did not get into this sport to fish under only these conditions. If you did, you will quickly find out that the best fishing from the beach usually takes place either under the cover of darkness or during the nastiest weather Mother Nature throws at us. I prefer a pullover style jacket instead of those with zippers as I haven't found a zippered one that will keep me dry under rough water conditions. For years I have been wearing Helly Hansen pullover tops and they still are my favorite for year round use in moderate conditions. If there are no mosquitoes present, wishful thinking on my part, I often will fish without a top in the summer months. When I am presented with stormy conditions and I have to wade to the far rocks or a sand bar where rolling surf is usually a norm, I prefer a jacket that has sealed cuffs on both the wrists and neck. Aquaskinz and Simms are currently the two leading manufacturers which provide these features. Dri-Core, a wonderful jacket manufacturer, is no longer in business. Some anglers to this day consider the Dri-Core jacket to be the ultimate neoprene top. If you question whether you really need a jacket with a sealed neck and cuffs then you have to ask yourself do you really want to stay dry? No surfcaster that I know, young or old, has not taken a spill at some point even on a flat sandy beach and gotten home soaked. Can you live without it? Certainly if you plan mostly to fish sandy beaches during the day and you will hang up your gear as soon as the first cold front makes its way from Canada in the fall. Then you don't need this type of gear. But if you are intent on standing toe to toe with an angry sea in the middle of the night and you put a premium on the ability of the jacket to keep you dry and warm, then you should invest in one. The jacket also acts as a barrier against a biting wind and it will keep your body heat within the jacket much better than if you opt for only layers of clothing. Regardless of how many layers you put on, if you get them wet it will short-circuit your trip in a hurry. Jackets should always be worn over the waders and never tucked into them. A wader belt should be worn over the jacket, preventing water from getting under it while you wade or even worse, while you are knocked off you feet by a wave.

WADER BELT

I might sound like a broken record by now, but again I must implore you to choose quality over price when picking your belt. Considering the gear you will carry on your belt and its replacement cost, you will see immediately why you should insist on quality construction. The most important feature is a good buckle that will keep the belt in place regardless of your body motion. Secondly, the buckle should be easily opened in case of an emergency. If you are swept into deep water and you must shed your waders in a hurry you will have no time to fiddle with your belt clip. One squeeze of the buckle or a pull on a clip should release your belt immediately. Stay away from Velcro fastened belts as with time they wear and they will open unexpectedly when you bend down to do something, like grabbing a fish to land it.

SURF BAGS

Every surfcaster, regardless of the type of fishing he does, back-bay or ocean front, needs to have some kind of contraption to carry his lures, pork rinds and extra leaders. Today there are many lure bags available in all shapes, configurations and sizes. A good surfcasting bag should be made out of water shedding material and built sturdy to withstand a harsh saltwater environment. The bag that might be a "bargain" in terms of cost can quickly turn into a nightmare if you are forced to lug a

Some of today's most popular surf bags from Hunter, Aquaskinz and Van Staal.

water logged piece of junk on your shoulder for a long period of time. When choosing a model or configuration, pick one that best suits your fishing style and needs. If you like to embark on your expeditions with only a few lures get yourself a single row bag. If you are like me and are always afraid of not having a particular lure when I need it, the two row model might be better suited for the way you fish. In either case I prefer bags that have side pockets in which I can carry an extra spool filled with line. There are few things worse than making an hour long trek over boulder strewn terrain only to run into problems and need to replace the spool on your reel. In addition, a pocket for pork rind is preferable although not a necessity. Aquaskinz makes a very useful pork rind holder that attaches to your surf belt. Another important feature that I personally crave is a lot of inserts for storing bucktails inside the bag. Whatever style or manufacturer ends up being your final choice, make sure that the flap that folds over the bag has a lot of Velcro and is not easily opened. Regardless of your skill level you will take an occasional tumble in the surf, it happens to the best amongst us. Having a strong Velcro closure will go a long way towards keeping your bag closed and your lures safe. Trust me, if you think that you will have the time to secure the bag during your tumbling in the surf, you won't. You'll most likely do what I do, fear for your life and just hope to regain the footing on terra firma before swallowing a gallon of seawater. Your lures will be the last thing on your mind while you are getting tossed by unforgiving waves like a sock in a dryer.

I personally like Van Staal bags and have been using the same two-row bag for many years. Aquaskinz has found many fans in recent years with their constantly evolving line of fine products. Their bags are very durable and well designed. Hunter Surfcasting Gear has a bag that could be considered the "ultimate" surf bag with hand stitched seams and made out of water shedding sail canvas. These three brands are considered the best of the breed in this category but since there are no patents on plug bag design, many competitors have cropped up in recent years with bags similar and in some cases almost an exact copy of the before mentioned models. As with anything else, use your friends as a sounding board and get their advice on which bag and configuration they prefer. Sometimes paying a few dollars more is well worth it because of the quality of the components that go into making a superior bag.

There has always been considerable debate amongst the ranks of surfcasters in regard to which inserts are better: square or round? I always preferred round ones but this might be more of a habitual thing than anything else. Personally, I don't think you can go wrong with either design providing that the tubes are made out of a quality material that will not react with soft plastic lures. In addition, the inserts should be able to withstand the harsh saltwater environment. If the inserts look and feel like they will not last, you will regret your purchase pretty fast as you will end up with another bag that will gather dust in your garage. I would suggest following the advice of your friends on specific brands and pay a little more to get a quality bag. After all, a good surf bag should last you for many years while a cheaper version might fall apart after a single season of fishing. In the end the more expensive bag just might end up being a bargain.

PLIERS

There are few items that are attached to a belt of a seasoned surfcaster, none more important than a good pair of pliers. Whether you treat yourself to the fanciest titanium model or you opt to go with something that won't break the bank, you should make sure that the pliers you buy have a cutter, won't rust and you can apply enough power to cut through a hook. Most of the manufacturers that cater to saltwater anglers include all of these features in their products. They must be rustproof for obvious reasons as saltwater will corrode cheap pliers after a single trip. You will need a cutter to cut your braided line, mono or a leader and in an emergency, even a hook that finds itself imbedded in your clothing or worse your hand. I also want my pliers to be able to grip the hook with authority and I do not want to be concerned that it may slip while I am unhooking a fish. I have been using the seven inch Van Staal pliers for many years and although they are pricey, I can honestly say they are one item in my arsenal that I never regretted buying. There is something to be said about having confidence in your pliers while standing waist deep in the water, in pitch darkness, trying to unhook a thrashing bluefish and doing

this while getting knocked about by waves. There are many models on the market today from various manufacturers. Abel, Donmar, Accurate, Shimano, Van Staal and others make quality pliers that should last you a long time. Of course, Manley has a pair that has been one of the favorite tools of many generations of surfcasters. I would advise that you stay away from pliers that

No surfcasting outfit is complete without a surf belt. It helps in keeping the water from entering your waders and it also serves as a tool carrier.

are designed for delicate tasks like tying flies as they generality do not generate enough force for cutting through a hook.

EXTRA STUFF

In addition to pliers you might want to carry a few tools to help you in landing, unhooking or weighing fish. Today's angler is very much aware of the collapse of the striped bass fishery in the late 1980's and the conservation ethic runs strong in the surfcasting community. Days of piling fish on the beach destined for the fish markets are a distant memory and today's angler is well aware of the need to conserve the resource for the future generation of surfcasters. In recent years the "lip gripper" tools have enabled us to unhook a fish without ever laying a hand on it and in the process preserving the protective layer of slime that covers the fish's body. This slime actually protects fish against bacterial attacks and the less we handle them during the release process, the better are its chance of full recovery after being returned to the water. I have used a Boga Grip tool for a long time now and found it to be indispensable especially at night. It makes it easy to use one hand to grip the fish's jaw with the Boga and the other to use the pliers to remove hooks. This is ideal as it keeps your hand away from the fish's teeth and from the swinging trebles on a thrashing fish. You can also keep the fish in the water during the process.

Another tool that takes very little room on the belt is a hook disgorger. This ingenious tool is nothing more than a handle with a straight piece of heavy wire with a half turn in the shape of a hook on one end. Occasionally a fish will swallow a hook or a plug and you will have a hard time getting your pliers around the hook in order to remove it. With this tool all you generally need to do is put slight pressure on the hook downward and it will usually come free.

I also carry a few stainless steel "D-rings" attached to my belt. These are another ingenious invention that can be used to either fasten other tools to the belt such as the pliers, via a lanyard or as a resting place for your rod when you need both hands to deal with a bird's nest or retying a knot. These are the only tools that I personally carry on my belt, but I have seen anglers who have so much gear attached to their belts one would think they were being parachuted into the Amazon wilderness to battle pythons.

Kidding aside, there are good reasons these anglers carry extra items on their belt and this usually has to do with the way they fish.

Those who fish live eels will usually have an eel bag attached to their belt. Others like to carry an extra bucktail holder, while some might have loops for securing their surf bag to their belts and a few, like my friend Bobby, like to still lug a steel chain stringer just in case the fish that so far has only appeared in his dreams decides to make an appearance when he is far from his buggy. Whatever tools you decide to carry on your belt make sure you attach it via a lanyard to the belt. I can't tell you how many times I have dropped my pliers or a Boga in the water or amongst jetty rocks over the years. Fortunately all my tools were attached via the lanyard, made out of coiled phone wire, and I was able to retrieve them with ease. Otherwise it would be a mighty expensive snafu.

Another item you should consider having attached to your belt is a sharp knife that will not rust when in contact with salt water. It has many uses but none more important than in emergency situations which might arise in the darkness. One of my friends, Edward, was wading at night at Montauk Point when he found himself entrapped in braided line that had been disposed of by an angler amid the rocks. Ed was unable to lift his feet from the entangled line and was being knocked about by the waves as he was unable to move his feet to establish a stable platform. While he steadied himself with the butt end of his rod, as if it were a cane, he managed to cut himself free with his knife and saved himself from a potential disaster.

JETTY TOOLS

Those who are fond of spending a lot of time fishing on jetties or other slippery rock piles have their own set of special tools that aid them in fishing, landing and releasing fish. First and foremost, they are concerned with their own safety. If you are planning to fish a jetty or any slippery rocks you have to invest in a pair of wading cleats to help you navigate this difficult terrain. I have to warn you, cleats will help you keep your balance to the extent that you will be able to get some traction on the slippery rocks but they won't make you invincible. They are just another safety item that helps us to navigate slippery rocks. However, be assured that if you decide to be a mountain goat and try to impress your buddies with your skillful rock jumping pirouettes you might find yourself in agony wedged between two rocks. I am trying to stress that these cleats should be used as a tool, not as a solution.

Jetty anglers often wear carbide studded sandals to aid them in navigating slippery rocks.

Cleats embedded in a sandal like slip-on over wader boots are made by Korkers. They are by far the most popular brand in this category and you might want to rinse them after each use to prolong the lifespan of the carbide studs. Should the studs rust or break they can be replaced. Always buy wading cleats bigger than your wader shoe size as they have to fit over the boot itself. In addition, after you fasten the sandal to the boot via either laces or buckle, wrap a few turns of duct tape around the boot in the middle of the sandal. This will prevent the sandal from slipping off your boot foot while you are wading onto the rocks or even worse, when you take a tumble in the surf. This might be a low-tech way to protect your gear but let me tell you it saved many of my trips over the years. If I had a dollar for every time I came back to my buggy only to find out that the only thing holding the sandal to my boots was duct tape well, let's just say I'd have enough money to buy a lifetime supply of duct tape.

Fishing on a jetty or while perched on a boulder is one of the most dangerous ways to catch a fish in the surf and I think fish might know this as they love to congregate in these areas too. Anglers that fish on jetties that are high above the water sometimes use jetty gaffs that can be extended to lip-gaff the fish. Sometimes it is too dangerous to scurry down to the water line in order to land a fish and under these conditions a jetty gaff is used to land a fish without putting yourself in harms way. I've seen some anglers carry long handled nets onto the jetty but I always found them cumbersome to use especially if you are like me and fish alone most of the time. The only exception I can think of is when you are targeting weakfish from rocks. I have had many experiences over the years of tearing hooks out of these magnificent looking fish while trying to land them from the rocks. Their name "weakfish" does not imply that they are weak physically or do not put up a decent battle when hooked. On the contrary, they are a great gamefish but they do have a weak jaw structure that tears easily when too much force is applied during the fight. This is the primary reason for the hooks coming out of their mouths. Therefore, it is not uncommon that after you lift them out of the water that they fall off the hook and land in between the rocks where it is virtually impossible to retrieve them. I personally can live with a few lost fish in the water, but to lose them in the rocks with no hope of returning them to the water is just too sad for me. Therefore, I leave it up to you to decide if you want to carry a big gaudy net. If you do decide to carry one, opt for one with a wide opening and telescoping handle so you can land any fish from the top of your rock, avoiding its banging itself into the base of the jetty when it starts to thrash wildly.

If you are considering spending a lot of time working the jetties you should think about wearing either a wetsuit or slickers with studded boots. These places can be very inhospitable to an angler and if you find your-self swept off the rock the water can exit through the bottom of your slicker.

LIGHTS

It is common knowledge that striped bass are nocturnal feeders and consequently the best fishing for them usually takes place under the cover of darkness. Making a transition from strictly daytime fishing to night time is not an easy one, as in the darkness we must rely on other senses more than our vision. Being able to "feel" what the lure is doing in the dark is something that comes from experience and although it might take some time to get used to it, it is not that difficult to do. Landing a fish on the other hand, at night, is for many anglers a problematic experience. Some of my friends whom I consider very good surfcasters undergo some sort of transformation at dusk and turn into first degree googan's. Not being able to see where exactly the fish is during the fight, the inability to judge its size or suddenly being unsure of their footing on the jetty are just some of the issues that often crop up. Fortunately, a little light from the right angle helps alleviate their fears and provides enough confidence in their own ability to turn back into the steady anglers that they appear to be in daylight. Granted, some of us are more comfortable fishing in the darkness than others and no degree of flashlight power will change that. Picking the right flashlight that will best suit your needs is almost impossible considering the dizzying array of models of all shapes and sizes that are on the market today. The most important features of the flashlight you chose are that it be water proof and rust proof. The size or shape is up to your discretion, although I would advise you to purchase one of the smaller size models. You are not going to make a lot of friends in this sport if your flashlight shines like a beacon. Flashlights are usually worn around the neck and if you lug a large one all night long you might end up with a sore neck the next day. Some anglers, such as yours truly, like to attach the light to a length of rubber tubing that can act as a lanyard around your neck. This can easily be done with rubber or surgical tubing that you can find in a craft or a tackle store. Cut enough rubber tubing so the light can fit comfortably around your neck. Put the two ends of the tubing on the opposite sides of the flashlight and secure them with electrical tape.

If you have an urge to "swim with the fishes" like my good friend Peter Graeber you better make sure you have top notch equipment.

Rigged in this manner the flashlight is usually held in the mouth during use. Others prefer to make a loop with heavy, insulated wire that can be twisted to position the light in the direction they need illumination. Both methods provide for hands free use and facilitate performing whatever needs to be done.

Recently, I have been using a LED light which attaches to my hat, a great little gadget but I wouldn't count on this to be my primary light. Why? Just as I was getting enamored with this particular light, a wind gust took my hat with the attached light and deposited it into the ocean. You should carry a spare flashlight with you, in your waders or inside your surf bag. Being miles away from your truck and standing alone on a rock a few hundred yards from the shore in darkness is tough. Doing so and having your light die with no spare will also make you remember all the names of your favorite Gods. I should know. I have been there myself.

There is also a constant debate amongst surfcasters whether shining a light onto the water spooks fish. I don't think we'll ever get an answer to this question unless a fish decides one day to write us a letter expressing how they really feel, but till then my opinion is that shining a light at the water cannot help your cause. I like to turn around, away from the water every time I use the light either when landing a fish or while changing my lure. If for no other reason, then you should do this as a common courtesy to those who are fishing next to you.

SOME MORE ESSENTIALS

If you think this a lot of stuff, well, we are not done yet. There are a few more things to consider, some seemingly unimportant but take it from me, their worth is immeasurable when needed.

First, you need some type of bug repellent. As you already read, mosquitoes and I have this love/hate relationship. They love to eat me and I just plainly hate them. Regardless of your affinity for or against the little blood suckers you should carry some type of repellent, especially on nights with no wind. Late in the season, after the first frost has wiped out most of them, it might be safe to venture in the dark unarmed, but before that I always carry spray repellent with me. Make sure that you don't spray it on the lures, line or the palm of your hands. If you do, wash your hands and try to remove the oily film from them otherwise you will transfer this stench onto your lure. I found a long time ago that fish will often be turned off for a period of time if you toss a lure that has received some sort of accidental repellent transfer so be careful with that nozzle.

You also should be carrying a leader wallet with extra pre-tied leaders, at least a half a dozen for a nights fishing depending on location. In rocky areas a dozen might be needed while on sand you can get away with less. In either case, tying leaders requires concentration and patience in order to tie and draw the knot perfect. In the middle of the night or during the mayhem of a daytime blitz is not the time to attempt tying leaders. Do this in the comfort of your home before you go fishing and then stick them in your surf bag.

My last suggestion is something most surfcasters would not consider part of their "essential gear" until they venture at night without it. Not knowing how much time has elapsed, when is the tide ebbing or when will the rip set up is a very important element in successful fishing. I am talking about a timepiece. I don't care if you wear a Mickey Mouse watch or Tag Heuer masterpiece; a surfcaster needs to have a waterproof timepiece in order to be able to estimate the duration of a tide, to know when the high and the lows are taking place or when the current is going to change direction or speed. Perhaps, more importantly it will tell you when to go home to catch your son or daughter's little league game.

CHAPTER THREE

— TOOLS OF THE TRADE —

C hoosing a rod to use in the surf might be the most difficult decision a surfcaster has to make. Unlike the boating angler who can literally get away with using a single rod under many conditions, surfcasters have special requirements. They might need a long rod to achieve casting distance or a short and sensitive rod to feel in touch with light lures during the retrieve. On occasion they may also need a short and stiff rod to toss big bucktails off of a jetty while other times they have to take into consideration the probability of using the rod as a cane when wading over slippery terrain. It is no wonder then that most serious surfcasters own a myriad of rods in different lengths with different weight handling and action characteristics. So rod choice truly becomes a highly subjective decision, based on many factors in order to make an educated choice.

If you are just starting in the sport your best bet is to go down to your local tackle store and ask for advice. Stay away from the warehouse type sporting goods stores. The guys behind the counter in local tackle stores will not

Long rods are often necessary on oceanfront beaches to reach fish on or near distant sandbars.

steer you the wrong way as they would like you to become a regular customer and not just a one time purchaser. Additionally, they will be familiar with all of the local fisheries and once you tell them what species you are targeting and where you will be fishing they will guide you to the right equipment. These stores and the people that staff them are very knowledgeable and they also know what the local sharpies use that allow them to be so successful. In addition to asking you what and where you will be fishing they will then ask you if you want an off the shelf rod (a brand name manufacturer) or a custom stick. This is a rod made for your intended application out of a rod blank made by a well know manufacturer. Custom rods will be a little bit more expensive and can usually be made for you at most major tackle shops. If the shop itself does not make custom rods they might know of someone that can do the job for you, so do not be afraid to ask for a recommendation. The advantage of a custom rod is that it is made for your intended application, the reel and line you intend to use with the rod and the placement of the reel seat according to the length of your arm. With off the shelf models, you will not get all of the features you are looking for and so there will be trade offs you will have to make. Custom rod builders take into consideration the quality of the guides, guide placement and the number of guides. The most critical guide is the gathering guide, the first guide on a spinning outfit. The size of the guide and its distance from the reel seat is dependent on the size of the reel spool on the reel you will be using. This distance is dependent on where the reel seat will be placed, which is dependent on the length of your arm measured from under your armpit to where your hand reaches on the blank. This distance provides for the best balance and comfort especially if you contemplate throwing plugs for hours.

If I was forced to pick one rod which would be a great starter rod and which is versatile enough in order to fish many different places without giving up too much in distance or sensitivity I would have to go with a ten foot, medium action rod. Since I mainly fish with rods made by Lamiglas, I feel comfortable about giving advice about them but there are many good rod manufacturers out there that are vying for your purchasing dollar. Manufacturers like St.Croix, Loomis, Tsunami, Seeker, Daiwa, Star, Penn, Breakaway and many others make well-regarded rods and have earned reputations for using quality components in their building process. In addition most of the manufacturers that cater to the surfcasting market offer incredible warranties on their products, something that is nice to know considering these items will cost you quite a few dollars. Keep in mind that surfcasting is probably the most demanding type of fishing there is and you really should not even be considering skimping on the quality of your gear. Don't be impressed with fancy "names" on the products as they only serve as a marketing tool for the manufacturers, they add nothing to your experience in the surf. Washington might be a famous name but naming a lousy rod by it doesn't change the fact that the rod is still junk.

Rods similar in characteristics to the Lamiglas 120 1M blank that I had made for me as a custom rod is a great all around stick. You can punch through the wind with some authority with lures up to 4 ounces and you will still be able to toss lighter lures as well. If you are going to be a jetty jock, a shorter rod, about 8 or 9 feet is usually preferred for a few reasons. The elbow room on the rocks is usually at a premium and longer sticks become unwieldy. In addition, shorter rods are usually stiffer and have more backbone which is usually needed to turn the fish away from the rocks. Casting distance is rarely a consideration on jetties as deep water is usually reachable with a short cast.

I spend a lot of my time on jetties and rocks and have come to the conclusion that in order to really maximize my efforts and present my lures in the most lifelike manner, I need to switch from spinning to a conventional

In calmer back bay waters smaller rods are often more practical in order to cast smaller lures with precision.

set up. First, conventional rods are usually beefier than spinning rods even when built on the same blank .These rods handle heavy eel skin plugs and big bucktails which I like to use much more easily than spinning rods. Secondly, I can control my lures much better than with an open faced reel, thumbing my line in the free spool position when needed, especially when I use bucktails and deep diving metal lips. Lastly, I am able to keep my rod tip down, angled towards the water, which helps my lures dig even deeper and makes hook setting easier on the jetties.

For ocean front beaches I prefer the Lamiglas 132 1 M blank made as a custom stick for me. The eleven foot blank is rated "M" for medium action. I find the extra distance I can achieve with this rod is desirable on ocean beaches yet I don't feel I give up much in the way of sensitivity when using lighter lures. It can punch a big bottle plug through the nastiest wind with ease yet I feel in touch with my lure when I toss 3/4 ounce bucktails. This stick is great for reaching the outer sand bars where the big ones prowl for food.

In the back bays, estuaries, harbors and other protected areas long rods are often unwieldy to use as most of the lures used in these parts are on the smaller side and lighter in weight. Rods in the range from 7 to 9 feet are perfect for these areas with lighter ratings, such as medium or even light action. These rods are preferred for tossing light weight 4 inch swimmers, tiny bucktails, paddle tails and small poppers.

If your intentions are to fish around bridges you will need a rod similar to a jetty stick at these areas. Although usually located in calm water, bridges feature very strong currents and many obstructions from which fish have to be turned away.

As you can see, there really isn't "one size fits all" rod length or rating, which can be used by surfcasters regardless of where they are fishing. Sometimes you will need light sticks to present tiny lures properly. At other times you'll need a beefier stick to punch through the wind to reach those fish that are feeding at the edge of a sand bar. Regardless which length and rating you end up purchasing, make sure it affords you enough sensitivity so you can "feel" what your lure is doing during the retrieve. After all a rod that can cast your plug a mile but wont provide you with the ability to feel the action of your lure is as useful as a long broom stick. Take it from me, I use to fish with one.

REELS

Northeast surfcasters suffered a major blow when Penn Reels decided to discontinue production of their wildly popular "Z" series of reels. These reels have been real workhorses in the surf for over forty years. They were affordable, made with simplicity, easily modified and a snap to fix.

The fact that they were moderately priced and parts were readily available only increased their popularity. I don't mean to sound like these reels were an answer to all our prayers, far from it. They had their issues from not liking to be dunked under water to unfriendliness with braided line on some models but they were affordable for most anglers. They had a proven track record of

There are many quality reels on the market today from manufacturers like Daiwa, Shimano and others but none has found better reception amongst the surfcasting crowds than the Penn 706Z and VS250 from Van Staal.

being able to tolerate harsh surf conditions and to fight big fish. Today's surfcaster might have more "choices" if you count how many brands there are on the market. However, considering surfcasting exerts so much strain on our tackle I think discontinuing the "Z" series is a major loss for our sport. Because most manufacturers consider surfcasting a "niche" market very little attention is paid to creating designs specifically for this type of fishing.

Fortunately, whenever there is a market that is underserved by major manufacturers, small companies have stepped in to fill this void. This happens in all aspects of our daily lives and surfcasting is no different. Van Staal reels were born out of the idea to create the best light weight, high line capacity reel that could withstand the rigors of salt water and big fish. If you have ever had the pleasure of using one, I think you'll have to agree they have succeeded in their mission. Today Van Staal reels, even though they carry a hefty price tag, are the preferred reel of choice for serious surfcasters. These reels are as maintenance-free as a reel can be and they so far have not just met my expectations but in some ways exceeded them. Fishing with a reel totally submerged under water is not even an issue any more, the reel and drag are waterproof, the drag is smooth and the reels have plenty of cranking power. You can even drop it in sand, rinse it in a wave and the reel will flush itself out, stuff you wouldn't even dream about doing with most other reels. The only issue some have with the reels is that other reels because of their elongated spool design can cast a few yards further. Frankly, I have yet to be out fished by a guy who can reach only a few yards further than me, so I find this argument without merit. I use a VS 250 and VS 275 on my 11-foot rods and I also use a VS 150 on my 7-foot stick when chasing after weakfish in the summer. Although these reels are not cheap, I look at them as an investment in the way I fish. They almost never break down and consequently I don't loose any time in the surf. I have used them for years with only annual maintenance needed and this in itself is very strange if you consider the way I fish. The "maintenance" of my gear is kind of a running joke in my club. Most guys rinse their gear, reels, lures and waders in fresh water after each trip or at least occasionally. Since my kids sleep above my garage, I refuse to wake them up in the middle of the night by washing down my gear and putting it away. As a result my gear spends a lot of time in the back of my truck unwashed and salt encrusted. If my reels see fresh water half a dozen times a year, that's a lot, yet they still perform perfectly. I don't know about you but I'll gladly pay extra for that kind or performance and dura-bility. Recently another manufacturer, ZeeBaaS, has entered into the mar-ketplace with reels that many feel will become the new gold standard on the beach.

Daiwa, Penn, Shimano, Mitchell, Tica and others make spinning reels that are also popular with the surf crowd. When it comes to conventional reels Abu Garcia has earned a reputation as one of the most dependable revolving spool reels on the market and is my personal choice. Penn Mag and Newell are also popular with most sharpies who prefer to use a reel that does not have a level wind. The reasons for this are many. Some guys use long leaders that are wound onto the spool and knots can get caught during a cast when they shoot through the narrow level wind opening. When fighting a large fish in those critical last few feet of the surf where undertow is at its strongest, the level wind may not let the line slide all the way onto the spool therefore increasing pressure on the line and knot. In addition, many feel that a level wind is just another thing that can fail so removing it technically eliminates one future headache. I find these concerns valid but not enough to make me remove my own level wind. I just can't see myself spending a whole night worrying if my line is spooling the right way onto the reel, especially when I am fighting a decent fish in the dark. However, I think paying a little attention during the retrieve goes a long way toward reducing any snafus with or without a level wind. Be careful when using light lures as the line will lay loosely onto the revolving spool because of the lack of tension. If you then switch to a heavy lure the line might come off the reel too fast creating the dreaded backlash. This is easily remedied before disaster strikes by either adding pressure by retrieving your line through pinched fingers or making a soft cast with a heavier lure first and making sure the line is going tight onto the spool before making a long cast.

LINE AND LEADERS

It is quite fascinating to look at what happened to fishing line in just the last ten years. We went from strictly monofilament to the early braided lines that were great at the time but pale in comparison to current offerings. Today's braid is thinner, more supple, with increased sensitivity and even less memory. I have to say, sometimes I feel bad for the darn fish with all the fancy gear we use today. From a surfcaster's point of view this may not be true as we can still only go where the legs will take us, but the boating angler has so many electronics at his disposal that I sometimes wonder how they can fail to catch a fish. Maybe their batteries died from all their gadgets? Kidding aside, today's surfcaster has some great tools at his disposal as well, none more important than a braided line. These super lines have brought the action of the lure closer to us than we have ever experienced before. With no stretch and increased sensitivity we can almost feel an impending strike before it ever happens. This in particular helps when working bucktails or other lead heads, as it is much easier to stay in the contact with our lures. Zero stretch makes strong sweeps of the rod unnecessary when setting hooks. Often just a strong flick of the wrist is enough to drive a hook through a fish's jaw. Because of their thin diam-

Quality line helps you load a rod to its maximum potential and enables you to cast lures further. Heavy leader material helps in shock absorption during a cast and offers better abrasion resistance against rocks or the sharp teeth of a fish than either regular mono or braided line.

eter, braided lines can be cast a greater distance than mono of similar test and with their lack of memory, wind loops are all but eliminated.

I tried different products over the years until I found Berkley Fireline and have been using it ever since. It has good abrasion resistance, it casts very well and the knots are a cinch to tie. No pun intended. I only use one knot to secure my braid to my swivel, a Palomar knot. The only modification I use when tying this knot, in comparison to a regular Palomar knot, is to thread the double looped line through the eye of the swivel twice before forming the knot. I feel that tied this way the knot is less likely to slip. Not that it ever has but I guess its one of those things you can chalk up to a habit. If you are new to the sport and are weighing the pros and cons of braid versus mono my advice would be to go with mono in the beginning until you get the hang of the casting and retrieving especially in windy conditions. Monofilament is much more forgiving than braid and easier on the tackle and the angler.

A word of caution about braided line. Braid will cut your index finger to the bone during the cast if you use a heavy lure, that's why most anglers tape their finger with some type of waterproof tape or use a finger guard. I have gotten away from using these finger aids and have been using Aquaskinz gloves instead for casting. These gloves are the most comfortable gloves I have ever owned, and the only ones I was ever able to use to tie a knot in the middle of the night with ease. Recently Aquaskinz added a Kevlar tip to the casting finger making this product even better.

In the interest of safety I want to mention something that is also very important to your well being, a leader. This short piece of either stiff monofilament or leader material is used not to protect the fish but the angler. It aids us in landing fish as it gives us something to grab onto when the fish is brought in close. Grabbing a braided line particularly with your bare hands is a very, very bad idea as the pressure the fish puts on a super thin braid will allow the braid to slice through your hands rather quickly. The leader also acts as a guard against barnacle covered boulders, the sharp spines of the fish or its gill plates. I don't believe that a Fluorocarbon leader is a necessity considering the water conditions we fish in but like anything else, there are exceptions. The waters in the northeast are full of plankton and bottom sediment and we rarely deal with crystal clear water. Under these conditions fluorocarbon is really a nice thing to have but not a necessity. However, fluorocarbon has better abrasion resistance than monofilament and its reduced visibility helps us present our lures more naturally in the calmer, clearer water of back bays. Most of the time I use 60 to 80 lb mono as a leader in lengths from 24 to 36 inches depending on the structure I am targeting and the elbow room available. A quality swivel attached via an improved clinch knot on one end and a # 54 Duolock snap on the other end attached via the same knot. The only time I use lighter leaders is with my 7-foot rod when I am chasing after tiderunners in the summer. As I am tossing tiny lures from 3/8 to 3/4 ounce, the heavy leader actually makes presentation difficult. So under these circumstances I often scale down and use a 30 or 40 pound test leader instead.

Braided lines made pencil popping an easy proposition.

There are some surfcasters who prefer to tie everything direct without using a snap. They feel that the snap can open under the pressure exerted by the fish or that the fish's jaws will crush it. A good friend of mine and one of the better surfcasters on the east coast, New York surf fishing guide Bill Wetzel, feels that in addition to all this he can work a bucktail in much more lifelike manner when tying directly than by using a snap. I'll agree that bucktails are one lure that do benefit from tying directly but I don't think the difference gained by doing this is worth the effort. I have no desire to cut and re-tie my leader every time I want to change my lure. Besides, I believe it is almost impossible for a fish to crush the snap. The snap would have to find itself exactly in the fishes jaw (something that rarely happens) and then it would also need to be standing in a vertical position to be crushed by pressure (something that almost never happens).

There is one thing that has cost many surfcasters a lure or two, including yours truly on occasion. However, it is the result more of operator error rather than equipment failure. Many times, especially when the fishing is hot, an angler doesn't take the time to check if the snap is fully closed after changing a lure. What happens is the next time a hook set is attempted the snap opens and becomes a straight piece of wire and of course there goes the fish and the lure. The angler does not realize this until he reels in the slack line, then he surmises that the snap failed. Of course, the failed snap will be shown to everyone who will listen, as to the size of the fish that caused this to happen, most likely, this "huge' fish will have been the fish of a lifetime. In the meantime there is a schoolie out there with a bucktail in its mouth. Don't laugh; this happens a lot more often than you might think. I like the convenience that the snap affords me and the few fish that I lost over the years were definitely the result of me not closing the swivel correctly instead of the fish crushing the snap. If you feel that the Duolock is too easy to open then go with Crosslock snaps. They are a little harder to get around the nose of some plugs, in particularly bucktails but they are also harder for fish to open.

HIRE THIS MAN!

A few years ago, I was fishing alongside of Vito Orlando, a dear friend and a bucktailer extraordinaire. We were working Caswells Point which is located about a twenty minute walk west of Camp Hero State Park in Montauk. There was a good heave in the ocean that day and we had bass on just about every cast using bucktails in conjunction with the white water. We were so engrossed in the action in front of us that we did not immediately notice three anglers that were wading out on the shallow reef looking for flat boulders to stand on. As I glanced to my left two of them were walking about twenty yards behind a lead guy whose body profile was very familiar. As they got closer I immediately recognized the lead person to be another extraordinary surfcaster, Montauk surf guide Bill Wetzel. I call him the "hardest working guide in the business" and he sure earned his nickname this day. Taking care of yourself under the bluffs on the south side is very hard; sometimes the waves build up and are so large you have no time to evade them. At times all you can do is just say a prayer and then duck, hoping no bones will be broken once you regain your footing ten yards down the beach. For a guide, trying to make sure your clients, who never waded onto rocks in their life, are safe is almost impossible. Bill got knocked around a bit while he looked for two flat rocks that his clients could stand on in relative comfort and safety. He wanted to put them into fish but since they were green he also did not want to see them get hurt. His clients wobbled over bowling ball rocks and boulders covered with kelp taking an occasional tumble until they finally got on the rocks he chose for them. Bill tied a bucktail directly to a leader for one guy and told him to cast it into the white water, which wasn't hard considering the whole darn reef was one big foamy mess. These guys were about twenty yards apart and now Bill was wading through the same unfriendly terrain to tie a bucktail to his other client's leader. Although his clients were safe on the rocks Bill had no such luxury as water was already up to his waist as he was wading and when a wave rolled over the reef he disappeared under it. A few moments later he resurfaced, his "lucky" hat stubbornly attached to his head. He shook the water off his Aquaskinz jacket and kept wading till he reached his other client. He then proceeded to tie a bucktail to his line, gave him the instructions and backed off a few yards onto a small rock in between the two of them. He was half way into the motion of making a cast himself when his first customer yelled that he was stuck in the rocks. Bill attached his bucktail back onto his guide and slowly waded towards his customer. The waves were getting bigger and for every two steps forward he was pushed back one. He was taking some brutal punishment and by the time he reached his client, he had already broken off his bucktail. Bill being Bill found himself directly tying a bucktail again all the while getting rocked by waves. I watched this in amazement and I breathed a sigh of relief when Bill yelled over the sound of roaring surf to his client to go ahead and cast. The guy leaned into his rod and made a cast but Bill did not get a chance to find a rock for himself when his other customer called that he was also stuck. As Vito and I watched in amazement Bill was again wading through the rough surf to set up his other client. This went on for sometime, Bill getting pummeled by the

Nothing is more rewarding for surf guide Bill Wetzel than seeing a smile on his customer's face after landing a fish.

waves, spending more time on his behind than on his feet, all to put his clients into some action. The fact that he insisted on tying his bucktails directly and forgo a snap made this day a very painful experience but if you know Bill, it's all in a day's work. Eventually both of these guys hooked up, simultaneously, and now Bill was standing in the middle coaching them both on how to land the fish, not knowing exactly which guy needed help more. As painful as this experience was for Bill, I think he'll be the first to tell you that seeing the large grins on his clients faces as they posed for pictures made it all worth while. Poor Bill was also unfortunately the official photographer and could not even get a chance to take a few casts before he got pummeled by the wave again. The most fascinating part was when Bill called them off the rocks after an hour or so and told them their "casting session" was over and they would now go look for some better fish in the dark. I think you'd agree that Bill could have saved himself a lot of punishment that day if he had just used a snap but if you knew Bill well enough you'd also know that wasn't even an option. He'd tell you either do it "right" or don't do it at all. This is why I call Bill the "hardest working guide in the business".

HOOKS

Hooks are often overlooked as an important part of a fishermen's equipment, but they shouldn't be. When you carry thousands of dollars of rods, reels, lures and other gear on each fishing trip it is not that unusual to forget about the hooks. If fact, I have a confession to make. As I write this book and this chapter in particular, I emailed it to my good friend Ed Messina for editing or as he would call it, to take the "Zenoism's" out of it. Only weeks later did I realize that I never wrote a single sentence about hooks. So, as you can see I too sometimes don't put as much importance on hooks as I should, at least in written words. But believe me in the actual act of fishing I put the utmost importance on this matter, sometimes changing hooks during a single trip because I wanted more depth from my lure or because I lost confidence in its hook setting ability. After all what is the only thing that will hold that fish attached to your fancy lure, that is attached to your fancy line which runs along your fancy rod and gets wound onto your fancy reel? That's right, a mighty hook. Years ago Mustad and Eagle Claw were the top names in the hook industry because of the variety of styles and shapes they made and for the treble hooks that are used on most of our lures. Today, that is not case. Many other manufactures have now entered this very competitive market and today's surfcaster has more choices than ever before. Be this as it may, I don't think having a dozen different brands on your lures will help you in any way. Find a hook that features the strength you desire, that is made for saltwater fishing and that is made out of material heavy enough to be able to withstand the pressure a large fish can exert. For me, the number one and only choice these days are 3X VMC 9626 Permasteel hooks. They are the only hooks I use on my plugs as do most of my friends. In fact, if a favorite lure does not come with VMC hooks I will replace the hooks with VMC's. These hooks come with hook shanks in two lengths, regular and extra short. The company also makes a 6X model (extra strong) but I have to warn you that the added weight of these hooks might change the way your plug behaves especially on smaller lures. There is one negative that comes with VMC Permasteel hooks, they only come in closed eye models so you are left with two options; either cut the hook and bend the eye open or use a split ring. For me this is a no-brainer and I don't use split rings unless there is a reason for it figuring that they are just another component that can fail during a fight. Cutting the hook for placement on a lure has two drawbacks. The first is that the smaller hooks (size 1 to 3/0) and those with the shorter shanks, when cut, will lie very close to the body of the lure so that when the fish hits the lure there is often no room for the fish to get its jaws over the hook point to penetrate the fish's jaw. The second is that cutting destroys the Permasteel protective coating that retards rusting so the hooks will rust quicker. You can prolong the life of your hooks by coating them with clear nail polish or rinse them with fresh water after each trip. As I am lazy I usually discard them when they start to show rust. Cut the hooks with either an 8 inch nipper or Manley pliers. Some anglers have resorted to using Dremel tools and many others employ fancier equipment to get a cleaner cut on a hook. About now you are thinking if I cut this hook am I not weakening it? Let me assure you that I never, ever had a VMC hook open on me regardless of the way I made the cut. Opening the hook for placement on your lure the right way is very important in order to prevent failure. Bend the cut eye by bending it to the right or left of the hook shank. Under no circumstances should you pull the opened eye away from the cut and the hook shank. Opening the slot sideways hardly weakens the hook whereas pulling it apart severely weakens the tensile strength of the hook. Use two pair of pliers or a vice to open and then to close the hook again. If cutting the hook does not appeal to you, then use split rings. Make sure you buy quality split rings. For small

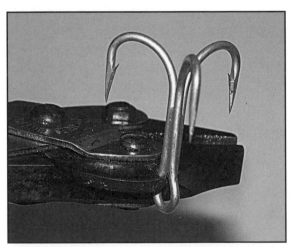

Cut VMC hooks as close to the shank as possible. Always open it by bending it either to the left or right of the shank.

plugs you can use 2/0's to 4/0's, while for larger plugs you can use 5/0's and 6/0's. Not all split rings are the same, be sure to get those that are rated heavy (H) as they are made from a thicker wire. Recently split rings with three turns of wire have appeared on the market. These are gaining in popularity and should be considered for certain applications. One of the keys in deciding what size split ring to use is to determine if the hook length in conjunction with the split rings causes the front and back hooks to touch each other or if the hook goes over the top of the lure and gets hung up. Whatever method you use make sure your hooks stay sharp at all times.

Thread the cut hook onto the swivel and bend it back into its original position.

Although some hooks are very sharp out of the package they get dull after a few good fish so carry a small file so that you can reestablish a good point. If this doesn't appeal to you, at least make an effort to check the sharpness of your hooks before you head to the beach. This will give you time to replace or sharpen the hooks before hitting the water.

CHAPTER FOUR

— TIDE, WINDS AND CURRENTS —

Any surfcaster who wants to be even moderately successful in the surf must learn how tides, winds and currents affect the areas he intends to fish. These factors will influence an angler's success rate more than any other factor, including the presence of baitfish, weather patterns or the time of the year. Fish are creatures of habit and they will return to the same locations year after year. Maybe their numbers will not be the same but that will depend more on the availability of food in the area than anything else. Once you learn which tide period is most productive, in a particular location, you can expect to reap the rewards of your scouting for many years to come. I said scouting because that is really what it will entail to learn a spot. Unless you join a club and information is passed on to you about a particular location or someone generously shares his knowledge, you will have to make numerous trips to that location during different stages of the tide to figure out what is the most promising period. When you narrow this down to a manageable time frame, you will now have to factor in the effect of wind and current on the structure you are targeting. Of

If you are planning to wade out to treacherous rocks far from shore you must have a good knowledge of tide and current periods.

course, one Nor'easter can rearrange the sand structure on a beach overnight and make all our efforts futile but that's the beauty of this sport.

The quest for knowledge should never end as structure and weather patterns are constantly changing. I look at this as a challenge to my fishing skills and not as annoyance as some do. After all, there are many productive places, particularly inside the inlets which have remained more or less the same for decades. Just so that we all know what I am talking about let us first describe what tide and currents are. Tide in general is the vertical movement of water and along the East coast it consists of 4 periods of approximately 6 hours in duration representing two rising phases and two falling phases. Each phase however, is slightly more than 6 hours. This explains why each rising (incoming) and falling (outgoing) cycle occurs about twenty five minutes later and fifty minutes later each consecutive day

The moon has a major influence on tides and its gravitational pull is primarily responsible for this great shifting of water from the bays into the oceans and back. Its effects are most pronounced during full and new moon periods when tides are at their highest level during the high tide period and lowest levels during the low tide period.

Wind direction and its strength can have an important influence on this highly choreographed routine. In the northeast, east winds will generally cause water to rise in the bays while west winds can have an opposite effect, creating exceptionally low tides in the same area.

A lot has been made about the importance of fishing around the new and full moon periods especially pertaining to the presence of large fish in the surf. Many articles and book chapters have been written on this subject and most have come to the same conclusion. Namely, there really is no hard evidence to support this idea. I find the periods around the new moon slightly more productive than normal which I credit to the nights being somewhat darker than normal and current a bit faster than usual. The full moon is great if you have a boat and can fish deep rips in the inlets or out in the ocean but for surfcasters the full moon is nothing but an annoyance. Yes, I've had a few good nights around the full moon over the years but I also have had ten times more that were just terrible with skies bright as day and water full of weed. This is another factor to consider when you fish during these periods. Because the water is higher than normal during new and full moons it floods the back bay marshland during the high tide. Once the waters start to recede, all the dead eel grass that has been decaying on the marshes gets washed into the channels and the current moves it towards the inlets making fishing often impossible during the period of outgoing water. However, I do not want to dissuade you from fishing these periods. The few days before and after a new moon remain my favorite time to fish during any month. I am just trying to point out some not so great things that will influence the action during these periods.

It is hard to generalize which tide period is better, falling or rising water. As I mentioned before too many things influence fishing in any area that a surfcaster cannot just count on getting the tide "right" in order to be successful. I do think it would be fair to say that most inlets and back bay areas are generally more productive during the time of outgoing water, with one exception to which I will get to in a moment. The reason why outgoing tide is preferred in these locales is simple. At high water the baitfish seek shelter in tidal creeks and marshes, darting amidst the eelgrass in shallow water. As the tide recedes the baitfish are forced to retreat from their hiding spots into deeper water. Here they encounter stronger currents which they will use to their advantage on occasion to travel around the bay but sooner or later they will get swept into a turbulent rip and lose all ability to control their movements. Stronger predatory fish will knowingly cruise these rips and pick off any baitfish that is helplessly drifting through the rip.

The exception to outgoing water being the preferred tide period in the bays and mouths of the inlet is when underwater structure lends itself to better water movement during the incoming tide period. For example, many of my friends fish the inlet jetties on outgoing tide as it's been the custom for decades. I prefer to concentrate on incoming in some of these same spots because I feel the rips "set-up" better on the flood. There might be a depression on the down tide side of the jetty that makes water "fall off" into the hole as it rounds the jetty creating some nasty and unstable water. Even though this spot is in the inlet and it goes against the grain to fish the "wrong" tide, I generally do better here than my friends. So don't be afraid to let water talk to you, let the water movement be your guide as to when to fish it and what to use.

HIGH OR LOW WATER?

If you ask surfcasters about the best strategy to fish ocean front beaches chances are you will be told that "high water out" is the most productive time. High water out is defined from the top of the tide through the first few hours of outgoing water. You will also hear that sandbars will act as a barrier during the low water period and it will preclude fish from entering the trough. This all sounds very reasonable in theory but I find that when applied in practice it leaves a lot to be desired. I've listened to this advice when I started out and followed it religiously only to find out that fishing the "wrong" tide is often the key to my success. Although each beach will have its own unique idiosyncrasies I find that the high water period to be a not so great time to fish many ocean beaches. The argument about the sandbar precluding the fish to coming close to the beach is overblown in my opinion as every sandbar has deep cuts where fish can comfortably enter and exit. In addition, during the period of high water the water column expands vertically providing more places for baitfish to hide and dispersing them. The last reason why I do not care to fish during high water is that often during these periods there will be very little or no white water rolling over the sandbars.

Big fish like this lurk in very shallow water.

There is also a school of thought about outgoing water draining the back bays and flushing the baitfish along the beach. This is absolutely correct except it's the current that actually channels the baitfish and not the tide. Current is the horizontal movement of water, while tidal shifts are the vertical movement of water. When water is higher in the bays than in the ocean, the water starts to pour out of the bays creating the currents. Since current usually runs about an hour to as much as four hours after the tide has turned this would leave us with a period when the tide is half way out before we can experience the benefit of the current. During lower stages of the tide a confluence of events takes place and in my opinion creates better opportunities for a surfcaster. First, we can wade out to structure that is off limits to us during high tide. Second, we get the benefit of a stronger current flow. Third, as the water over the sandbar gets shallower the white water rolling over it gets more pronounced uncovering invertebrates, clams and crustaceans from the sand. The fourth and in my mind the most important part has to do with bait concentration. As the tide is receding the bait must congregate in less and less water and this compression factor is much more appealing to the gamefish.

Let's take all these factors together and see if you find this appealing. You have white water providing cover for gamefish to come into shallow water, current to channel the bait and less water for them to congregate in. If you are a fish what is there not to like? If you say that fish might not enter the trough at low water because of the depth, I would point out that even at low water most of the troughs are deep enough to be un-wadable in order to get onto the sandbar. Since I've seen fish feed in inches of water and at times at my feet in ankle deep water, I find this argument without merit.

On rocky beaches strewn with boulder fields I also prefer the lower water period for similar reasons. During the higher stage of the tide the baitfish will seek shelter amongst the rocks in very shallow water but as the water recedes they will have to leave this protected area and move into deeper water. In addition a surfcaster can usually wade onto rocks much easier during the lower stages of the tide and have the opportunity to toss his lure into deeper water. I should mention that some rocky and sandy beaches are too far from the inlets to benefit from a current flow and the tide acts as a primary reason for movement of bait and fish in and out of these areas. Because of lack of current, I find these beaches to be less productive than the ones located closer to the source of the current. These beaches usually feature fish that are cruising for a meal instead of ones that are setting up feeding stations. If there is some white water rolling over the sandbars, you might have a shot of finding some feeding fish. However, if the surf is flat and there is no current, that beach becomes a very poor choice for tossing a lure. Without the benefit of current or the cover of white water, gamefish may be reluctant to cruise the shallow water and the period around high water is usually preferred on these beaches.

CURRENT OVER TIDE?

Unlike tide which is the vertical movement of water, current is the lateral or horizontal movement of water which is created by many factors, including the gravitational pull of the moon, the wind and the pressure that builds when large amounts of water are trying to squeeze through a narrow opening in the land. The best examples of this are areas around inlets, breachways and bridges. Although bridges don't seem to fit into a "narrow" passageway category as some have a very long span, they generally are built between two points of land closest to each in order to save on the time it takes to build them, material and general construction costs.

Beaches that do feature a strong lateral water flow, the current and not the tide will be the primary reason behind the movement of all marine life. In these places a surfcaster has to decipher how the structure is positioned in relationship to the current flow and what will be its effect on the structure itself. Regardless of what type of structure we might be fishing, there always will be one current period that will be more productive than another. If you know a spot where you can catch fish equally well during either current direction, please call me and I'll be right over! The key is to find what makes that particular piece of structure more appealing on a specific current direction. There might be a shallow rock reef with a deep hole on its side. This is the type of structure prevalent on Montauk's north side beaches. You may also find a shallow sandbar that curves towards the shore which benefits from inlet currents. This type of structure is typically found on the west sides of the inlets. On beaches that immediately border inlets or points of land that extend into the ocean, such as Sandy Hook in New Jersey or Orient and Montauk Points in New York, here is where you will find primary examples of the importance of current. In these places the current create rips as it encounters an obstruction in its path. The current wraps around or rushes over these underwater irregularities creating unstable, turbulent water. In most of these locales, the start of outgoing current and not the tide will bring the seasoned surfcasters into the water. As I mentioned before, there are always going to be exceptions to this rule and if structure is positioned in such a way where incoming current will have a more pronounced effect on fish movement, fish that period. Nowhere is this more obvious than under the fabled Montauk Lighthouse where a strong rip forms on incoming water. This spot is most productive during the last few hours of incoming water even though a hundred yards to the west and for miles in that direction the outgoing water is generally more productive.

Jetty anglers use inlet currents in conjunction with large bucktails when targeting big fish.

This section was only intended to give you a starting point, it is not meant to be cut in stone. If you have a place that works for you during the period of the "wrong" tide don't leave the fish and go in search of the holy grail. There are no "secret" spots and there is no right or wrong tide. The "right" tide is the one during which you catch fish.

SWEEP YOUR WAY TO SUCCESS

There are very few things a seasoned surfcaster finds more frustrating than getting up at the crack of dawn and peering out of the window only to find out that the wind is not as intense as he was expecting or worse, blowing from a different direction. You might ask why put so much emphasis on wind? After all, you are already up and the gear was packed in the truck the night before. So you might as well hit the beach, right? Wind direction and its intensity is often an integral part of how the structure you were planning to fish will set up. Wind affects not just the presentation of your lure but the length of your cast and the strength of the current. In addition, it can have an effect on the level of the tide and can act as the primary reason why the bait will be pushed offshore over the sand bar or onto the beach. I think that you'll agree that all those factors are very important to a surfcaster.

If all that wasn't enough, the wind can also have a very significant effect on the water temperature, sometimes more than the sun itself. Prolonged periods of southerly winds will bring the warmer waters on shore where northerly winds tend to have a chilling effect on the surf temperatures. Easterly winds tend to pile up water in the back bays often causing flooding in low lying areas where as westerly winds have an opposite effect. Since I did not write this book with any particular area in mind it would be hard to make general statements as to which wind is preferred. For example what works on Long Island's south shore that faces south, will have very little correlation with what happens on New Jersey beaches that face east.

Whatever the direction your beach might be facing, one thing that I can recommend with certainty and still sleep well at night is to fish that particular beach with the wind in your face. Once you get a wind from the direction you want now find a tide period during which the tide and the wind will move in the same direction. That is in my opinion one of the most important ingredients to finding good action on the beach, having the wind and the tide moving in the same direction. This creates a sweep or a current even on the beaches that usually don't have any and in the areas where current is normally abundant it makes water move even faster. Gamefish are very well aware of these occurrences and they will use them to their full advantage by slashing through these fast waters with ease while smaller baitfish are struggling.

Let's take a look at what transpires when the" wind + tide" scenario plays itself out on the eastern end of Long Island. Shagwong beach is located on the north side of the Town of Montauk and on the east side of the Montauk harbor inlet. Shagwong County State Park, as it is officially known or "Shag", as preferred by the regulars, is a fairly steady fish producer if uninspiring as compared to places a few miles east and around the fabled lighthouse rocks. Steady action with school bass and many more blues can be found along its length, particularly at the tip where a deep rip forms on outgoing tide. In late fall when the winds are out of the northwest they can put a chill in the air but they often warm the hearts of Shagwong regulars as they eagerly anticipate strong winds out of this direction and the strong currents they will create. Since Shagwong faces north, a northwest wind is coming slightly sideways from the left side. The dropping tide is also moving from left to right. The wind hits the beach at an angle and pushes the water towards the tip at a very fast clip, sweeping any baitfish that had the misfortune of finding itself along the beach. The water picks up in speed over the shallow bottom until it reaches the turbulent deep rip and usually all hell breaks loose. Some of the biggest fish of the year will usually charge the beach and take up position in the rip during this wind driven event. Once the winds have subsided, the larger fish will seek safety in nearby deep water rips while their smaller siblings will remain in their role as the day to day guardians of the beach.

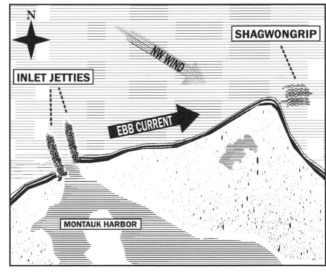

Wind and tide moving in the same direction often create good opportunities for surfcasters. On this drawing you can see that all the bait that is flushed out of Montauk Harbor during the period of outgoing tide will be swept east along the beach and into the rip at Shagwong Point.

Seasoned anglers know that strong winds coupled with a tide moving in the same direction will present possibly the best fishing of the year. Anticipate these events and I can assure you that if you make yourself a part of them, you will not be disappointed. A word of caution though, these kinds of events in the fall, be it a strong northwesterly on the drop or a nor'easter on the flood under the lighthouse attract many very experienced and confident anglers, along with a few googans like me. So-called elbow room will be at a premium and light tackle is a definite no-no, so make your plans accordingly. Think strong rods, big bottle plugs, loaded needlefish and of course, large bucktails.

NOR'EASTERS

Nor'easters are usually big events in the way they influence fishing along the whole east coast. These storms are usually massive in size and move very rapidly over the area. Before the storm reaches its crescendo, ocean beaches often light up as gamefish put on the feedbag just before the storm. We don't know if they anticipate churned water and the inability to feed in the eye of the storm or they are just taking advantage of the rough conditions the storm is creating. Whatever the reason, it has been documented that just before a nor'easter hits an area, the fishing dramatically picks up. Once the storm has settled over the area, the open beach-

Strong Nor'easters often produce remarkable catches on the north side of Montauk Point. Again, the key is to fish the period when wind and tide are moving in the same direction.

es become very difficult to fish as a very fast sweep is created. However if you move close to an inlet or fish within the confines of the inlet itself, you will find that this area remains very fishable throughout the storm.

The question now often becomes how much rain the storm is going to dump on us and what effect this will that have on the clarity of the water? Sometimes in cloudy water, chartreuse or parrot patterns work well on lures and bucktails but I have to be honest, muddy water is not my favorite type of water to fish. More often than not I have been left standing on the shore, watching bass and blues marauding schools of bait on the outer edge of the sand bar where the water was cleaner. Those with experience will hit the rips inside the inlets at night with large diving metal lips, giant pikies and big plastic shads. The best fishing of the year often takes place around these nor'easters, sometimes just before it, sometimes during and other times in their wake. Years ago it wasn't uncommon for action with large fish to last through the whole storm. Sadly that kind of action rarely ever happens these days. Once the storm has moved on and the winds have abated it's time again to hit the beaches. I do implore you to be very careful as the wave heights can be of gigantic proportions and it might take a few days before it gets back to normal. The rough water has a tendency to expose thousands of clams in the surf and where there is free food you can bet your last dollar our friend the striper will make an appearance. Heavy tins, large bucktails and bottle plugs are about the only thing that you can work properly over these big sets of waves until the water calms down.

Again, I must remind you to be very careful if you fish before, during or after a nor'easter. These storms tend to produce very large waves and because they are powerfully driven onto the beach the surfcaster often feels that he has to get closer to the water line in order to make a good cast. I have been suckered into this many times as the wave recedes. I usually take a few steps forward only to momentarily find a mountain of water sweeping me down the beach. Be careful out there, no fish is worth your life.

ONSHORE WINDS

The aforementioned events were examples of extreme weather conditions having a major impact on fishing the beaches in the northeast. If you are not enamored of the idea of casting into gusty winds or standing in a downpour you are not alone. Very few anglers can deal with these adverse conditions and I have been known to make a fool of myself on many occasions. What can I say? If you put me in a confined area where I am rubbing elbows with other surfcasters while a 40 mph wind is trying its best to take my lure and shove it back in my face, stuff does happen. Fortunately, most of the year a surfcaster is presented with light winds and moderate surf. Even though these stable weather periods and wind patterns might seem mild in comparison to a nor'easter they still have a lot of influence on fish behavior in the surf. As a general rule I always prefer to fish a wind in my face, regardless of what region or structure I might be fishing. On-shore winds drive the water over the sandbars creating a nice foamy roll of white water in which gamefish often find cover. Stripers in particular will always prefer to feed in highly oxygenated white water compared to calm water. Rolling white water unearths the crustaceans and tumbles whatever bait happens to be present in the troughs. I'll discus exactly why I think this is important in the chapter about beach structure. Getting back to the on-shore winds, they have a tendency to push the bait closer to the beach making a long cast often unnecessary as gamefish will follow the baitfish into shallow water. Some surfcasters hate winds that come at them because they reduces the length of their cast but they give very little thought as to what is transpiring in front of them in regard to bait and fish movement. On-shore winds are the straw that stirs the drink, the winds that bring the beach to life and should be regarded not as an adversary but as a welcome event. In fact, a stiff onshore breeze is probably a surfcaster's best friend.

WIND AT YOUR BACK IS GREAT FOR SAILING A KITE...

Winds that come directly from one's side, also called crosswinds are probably the most difficult to fish. They create a big bow in the line and sometimes a modification to the casting direction is necessary in order to present your lure in a halfway decent manner. Instead of a cast going slightly with the wind, you might have to cast directly into the wind in order

On calmer days, when wind is not a factor look for current to be the primary reason for bait movement.

to eliminate slack in your line. Frankly, I hate cross winds and if I can avoid fishing during these times I do. Either that or I find a location where I can use the wind to my advantage.

This brings me to another point. Don't fall in love with any piece of ocean structure and show up there and pray that the wind will shift to benefit your presentation. Don't make plans according to where your buddies are planning to be but instead look to turn the current wind direction to your advantage.

Although crosswinds are difficult to fish, I must admit that I like wind at my back even less. Yes, my casts sail half way to Bermuda but these winds also push baitfish over the offshore bars and out of my reach. In addition, they flatten out the surf taking away the precious cover fish crave in order to sneak into shallow water. I try to avoid fishing these types of winds on sandy beaches and instead concentrate my focus on the inlet rips which are not affected as severely by the direction of the wind. I don't find wind direction as important in calmer backbay water as its velocity. Many of these areas are very shallow and feature muddy bottoms so any prolonged period of strong wind will turn this water into the color of coffee. I prefer little or no wind here. If anything, I like a light "over the shoulder" breeze that helps me cast tiny plugs a little further and keeps the mosquitoes out of my face. Of course, the wind here can act as a double edge sword because of the small lures I usually use. If it is anything more than moderate and blowing in my face, I have no choice but to alter my plans. This is where having a fallback option comes into play. Every surfcaster should have at least one spot that they know will be productive on a particular wind. This way they always have a location to go to, regardless of wind direction. Over the years I have been fortunate enough to find my own little local nooks and crannies to the point that regardless of what wind Mother Nature blows at me I feel confident that I can work it to my advantage. Every wind except pure west! Try as I may I have yet to find a place where a hard west wind helps me in any significant way. As frustrating as that might be, it in a way adds to the mystique of this sport. No one is born with knowledge; no one has someone else making their casts. Through experience we learn and that is what makes this sport so satisfying. Deciphering wind, tide and current patterns with no aid of fish finders or sonar is the way my grandfather did it and I would bet yours did too. We are just continuing the tradition.

CHAPTER FIVE

— STRUCTURE —

Surfcasters in the Northeast are blessed with hundreds of miles of beautiful sandy beaches. However, very few locations along this shoreline can be counted on to be productive areas to catch fish. In fact most of it is just a sandy barren desert, devoid of marine life and much more appealing to a swimmer than a fisherman. Those few precious spots that do attract fish depend on the underwater sand structure remaining constant through the year. This is always an iffy proposition. Most of the ocean facing beaches in the Northeast share a common characteristic: a sand bar that runs parallel to the shoreline. In some places it might be reachable with a short cast while in others it might be a few casts away. Regardless of its distance from the beach, a sand bar is a most important piece of structure for a surfcaster. These structures created by nature are prone to be reconfigured after each storm. At times this can happen overnight. Therefore, a surfcaster must do his due diligence after each blow and hit the beach to re-familiarize himself with any changes that might have occurred.

The deep area between the sand bar and the beach is known as the trough and this is where most of the action takes place. Some very sharp anglers are of the opinion that these types of beaches are best fished around high water because at lower

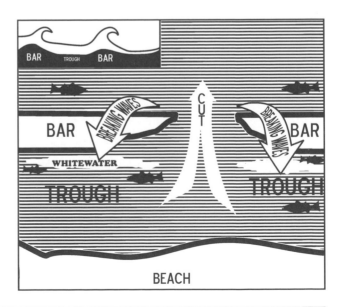

stages of the tide the shallow sandbar serves as a barrier to gamefish which want to enter the trough. I think this is a reasonable theory but I am not sure I agree with it for several reasons. First, at high tide the water column expands vertically, giving baitfish more room to scatter and hide. This makes them less attractive to predatory gamefish who like their feeding to be easy and their prey plentiful. They do not like to expend a great deal of energy chasing scattered prey. As the tide drops, the baitfish are forced to vacate their protective surroundings and retreat into the deeper parts of the trough. In addition, the contracting water volume congregates the baitfish which now seek safety in numbers. These same gamefish which a few hours ago were disinterested in chasing bait all through the trough have now changed their tune as the baitfish are crowded into confined places. This is too tempting for them to pass up. But how are they going to get over the shallow sandbar? First of all, rarely is the sand bar totally exposed even at low tide. I've seen bass and blues swim and feed in inches of water I don't think the sandbar impedes their desire to chow down on some food. Even if the sand bar was really shallow and the gamefish needed a sure-bet outlet to head into deep water, there usually is a solution to that problem. A "cut" is a hole or gap in the bar. The surrounding water on both sides is shallower than in the cut itself. You can easily identify these cuts, particularly at low tide, by looking for water that is a darker shade of blue compared to its surroundings. In these cuts the waves usually do not break until they reach the actual beach. These cuts are used by gamefish to enter and exit the trough at all times but particularly during the lower stages of the tide. Working these cuts with a large pencil popper at dawn by casting up tide and let it swing through the cut is very productive while at night the same technique will work with a needlefish. You might be surprised by two locations that I specifically target if I feel that fish are in the trough. One is the white water that is rolling over the sand bar while another is the lip of the beach where the sand meets the water, especially if the drop off in this location is pronounced. Both of these places share similar characteristic. They both take constant pounding from the waves, their bottom is continuously stirred up and many crustaceans are exposed which become an easy meal for a cruising predator. For this reason, I will make my first cast diagonally from the dry sand particularly at night before I set my foot into the water. You'd be surprised just how many fish, stripers in particular, lie close to the beach under the last wave that hits the shore, looking for any morsel of food to be dislodged from the sand. Then there is the white water that rolls over the sandbars with any onshore breeze. In my humble opinion, learning how to take advantage of this white water and fish it effectively will increase your catch more than any other technique. Let me take you down memory lane for a moment and show you why I put such importance on the simple tumbling action of the waves.

WHITE WATER

White water created by crashing waves serves as a primary hunting ground for stripers and blues along oceanfront beaches.

On a crisp fall day I stood perched on a rock on Montauk's south side, sight casting to a school of fish which, if they were any closer, would have been behind me. They were gorging on massive schools of "white bait" or bay anchovies. Regardless of what I threw at them the fish wanted no part of it, they ignored each of my plugs with the same maddening indifference. Out of more than a hundred anglers lined up shoulder to shoulder, I may have seen a dozen fish landed the whole afternoon. Considering that an acre of bass was rolling around at my feet, I could have done better using a net and scooping them up from my rock. The next day the same scene happened and after about an hour of stripers ignoring everything I threw at them, I decided to leave and fish the next rocky point. It was more to get away from the crowds than it was to catch a fish. I figured I couldn't do any worse there than here where the fish seemed like they were going belly up laughing at me as they rolled through the schools of bait. I thought that maybe, just maybe I could entice a fish to strike if I found a place with less baitfish present. Talk about irony! All the time we spend looking for bait in order to find predators and there I am walking away from it all. You could say I did not feel very good about my competence at the moment.

After a treacherous half-hour hike over some very unfriendly boulders I arrived at the next point and waded out and climbed up on a rock. I attached a Yo-Zuri Surface Cruiser and let it fly. I was relieved in a way to finally make a long cast instead of trying to "pitch" my lure to the fish swimming around my feet. My pencil popper was dancing a hundred yards out when the water exploded around it. Unfortunately the striper completely missed the hooks but this gave me the confidence I sorely needed. So the next hour I spent trying to tear my rotator cuff by making long casts in the area where I raised that fish but with no results. At this point I was ready to pack it in.

As I was removing my lure from the snap, I glanced at the water a few feet in front of me. A most peculiar thing happened. A large wave had just rolled over the shallow reef and milky, white foam was left in its path. Through the foam, erect dorsal fins of bass cruised. First one, then two, three and then too many to count. By the time I attached a small bucktail to my snap, the fish were gone. I made a dozen short casts in the area, which wasn't more that 20 yards away but drew a blank. A few minutes latter another strong wave came rolling through with white water blanketing the surf. The fins rose again and slashed through the foam yet as soon as the foam started to dissipate they disappeared. Again, I excitedly cast into the area and again I did not get a bump. Something clicked in my head, I opened my bag and pulled out a small metal lip plug and attached it to the snap. I stopped casting and watched the water for a few minutes trying to confirm the notions that were now spinning in my head. Sure enough, as soon as the water would foam up behind a wave, stripers would appear like clockwork and within seconds they would be gone. I timed the next wave perfectly and made a short cast right behind a cresting wave. I did not get a chance to work the lure an inch before it got hammered. I landed the fish and still unconvinced, made another few casts in the general area but again, nothing was there. I was however keeping my eye on the next set of waves coming at me and made sure my lure was out of the water and ready to cast as the wave approached. I made another cast to the backside of the wave, right in that frothy water and as soon as my plug showed movement not one but two stripers went after it. This went on for the whole afternoon, standing there all alone catching fish by only casting at the foam. I won't lie, I tried to sneak in a few casts when there was no white water showing but I drew a blank every time I tried it.

I walked back like a little kid with a spring in my step after a few hours, forgetting completely about the bowling ball sized rocks under my feet. After getting back to the point which I left in the morning I asked my friends who decided to stick around how they did. Their long faces gave me the answer to my question. It looked like today's session proved to be just as frustrating as yesterday's. Then a friend said "I didn't have any fish but Don Musso, the legendary plug maker of Super Strike Lures was killing them on metal lips which he was casting from the shore. His plugs landed not far from the rock I was standing on. I tried a metal lip too but only got one bump when my plug was behind a wave in the white water and I couldn't

White water is the straw that stirs the drink. More turbulence creates better opportunity for bass and blues to feed.

really see it." Oh really? That day was my "epiphany" moment, a day when I stopped casting pencil poppers a mile off the beach. A day after which I knew I would never look at white water rolling over the sand bar or a shallow reef the same way again. From that day on I become obsessive about trying to understand the formation of the waves, their effect on fish feeding behavior and more importantly on how water movement affects the presentation of my plug. I concluded that stripers in particular love to feed in the white water that is generated by a rolling wave. As the wave reaches a shallow sandbar it builds up in height and starts to tumble, picking up speed as it barrels toward the shore. Whatever baitfish or crustaceans that happen to find themselves in its path get helplessly tumbled within the wave. Once the wave crashes the baitfish are temporally stunned, floating on the backside of the wave. The stripers know this and trail the wave as it builds up speed. They then move in to feed while the white, foamy water acts as a cover, disguising their presence. As the wave recedes back into the ocean they retreat along with it to deeper water. This highly synchronized feeding takes place right under the noses of many surfcasters but they never notice it as they cast their lures a hundred yards past the feeding fish. I want to stress that this kind of feeding is not limited to the fall run. It also happens in the daytime or at night. This is how these gamefish feed to survive. Think about it. White water provides all three things that are of utmost importance to gamefish. First, cover and ability to stealthily get in and out of the shallow water without being detected. Second, plentiful food unearthed by each wave in the form of crabs, sand fleas and other crustaceans. Last and most important, being in position to ambush and feed on helpless bait without expending much energy in the process. I can't think of a piece of structure where gamefish are in a better position to hunt with ease than white water.

For a surfcaster the most appealing thing about this occurrence is that all this takes place generally within casting range of any plug in his bag, including the metal lip swimmer. In fact the metal lip swimmer is probably the deadliest lure to use in conjunction with white water. Timing my casts, so that the metal lip lands on the backside of the wave has produced countless numbers of bass and blues for me over the years. But metal lip swimmers are not the only lure I find to be very effective in the white water. Quite the opposite! Most lures become more productive under these conditions. Bucktails in particular have always produced better catches when white water is present. In fact, I changed the way I retrieve most of my lures in order to take advantage of the opportunities that white water creates. When casting a bucktail, it is not as necessary for it to land in the foam but it's still important to cast behind the wave. If your lead head lands in front of the wave the chances are the wave will collapse on it and you will loose contact with your lure temporarily. By the time you regain contact the bucktail will most likely be out of the productive water. What I like to do is cast a bucktail behind a wave and then quickly drag it into the foam. Once in there I'll try to slow down my retrieve and keeping it behind a wave as long as possible. Eventually I will lose the wave as it moves a lot faster than the bucktail should be retrieved but then another set of waves will come and I'll try to position my bucktail so it slides over the next wave and into the white water again. When conditions allow, I like to wade out a little deeper than I usually do and then cast parallel to the shoreline in the white water. When casting in this direction you can often work a metal lip swimmer on a single wave all the way to the shore. Another lure I love to use in conjunction with white water is a needlefish. When I plug the open beaches at night, the needlefish is usually my "go to" lure. I like to manipulate my retrieve so I can hold the needlefish in the roughest part of the wave as long as possible. After reading all this some of you still might not be convinced that white water is the most important key to success when plugging ocean beaches. After all, these beaches extend as far as one's eye can see. Why would gamefish concentrate and congregate on such a small sliver of beach? I implore you to look at the big picture. Most of the planet we live on is covered by water yet most of the marine life is found in a narrow band of inshore waters. On ocean beaches, that tiny sliver of white water rolling over the sandbar presents a gamefish with an opportunity to satisfy its hunger by virtue of its strong swimming ability in a place where other creatures can't maneuver. It affords them cover to come into the shallow water unnoticed yet they are only a few strong swipes of their tails away from the safety of deeper waters. Human behavior is not much different as we too congregate in places where food is easily obtainable and shelter is in close proximity. We leave the vast, wide open wilderness to animals. Imagine a deer hunter, not comfortably camouflaged in the tree but instead running after a deer in the wide open field. I think we all can agree he would most likely go home hungry. Gamefish don't hunt for the sport of it, they do it for their basic survival and as such they cannot expend more energy hunting down prey than they would gain it by eating it. White water creates the opportunity for them to do just that, feed with an advantage over other species with minimal effort and maximum results.

MORE OCEANFRONT STRUCTURE

There are a few other types of structure on sandy beaches that game-fish find attractive and while I don't think any are as productive as white water, they do hold fish at certain times. Jetties that jut into the water in some places every few hundred yards attract some resident fish all year while others such as sandy points and bowls are most productive during fall months. I know it seems like too broad a statement to make but I always make a few casts parallel to a jetty before I ever put a foot on the rocks. I can't tell you how many times I have found stripers cruising tight to the jetty in some very shallow water. In addition, the "pocket" of any

jetty can be often more productive than the jetty itself. In the fall when bait is plentiful along the open beaches, gamefish like to trap their prey in the pocket of the jetty where the rocks and the beach meet. One school of predators at the tip of the jetty stops the bait-fish from rounding

Jetties always receive a lot of attention from surfcasters. These man made structures provide many ambush opportunities for gamefish and feature a lot of marine life who call the crevices amongst the rocks their home.

the jetty tip while others take turns slashing through the schools of bait trapped in the pocket.

Early in the year I find that small swimming plugs and bucktails are most effective as most fish found around these jetties will be on the small side. However inlet jetties, where fast currents usually attract bigger fish, will require you to use larger lures. As with anything else in the sport of surf-casting there are exceptions and for a week or two during the month of June the larger fish usually move in to the vicinity of these rock piles. Rigged and live eels and metal lips fitted with eel skins are most produc-tive at this time when big stripers are looking to feed on resident blackfish that call these rocks home. At dawn I like to work metal lips or small pencil poppers as tight to the rocks as possible and across the tip of the jetty. Remember, the water adjacent to these oceanfront jetties is fairly shallow and large, noisy pencil poppers might actually spook the fish instead of attracting them.

Few sandy beaches are straight and narrow. Most have a series of points protruding into the water with deep water coves on both sides of the points. Whether they protrude deep into the water or not they can be very productive areas. Small rips can form around these points and strong turbulence can develop on its shoals. The gamefish do not need much of a divergence in the bottom structure in order to use it to their advantage and nowhere is that more evident than here. A small depression on the side of the point can be used as staging areas for stripers as they wait for bait and crustaceans to be washed over and through the turbulence on the point. Or they might periodically dart into the white water to feed and then return to the hole to rest where the current or sweep is not as pronounced, thus saving their energy. All these little nuances can be exploited by the surfcaster who is willing to explore the area and not just concentrate on casting big poppers a hundred yards off the beach. If you are willing to accept the theory that in the surf nothing is constant and learning experiences don't terminate at the end of the tide but last for a lifetime, you'll do well. Stay humble and become a student of the sport and I can almost guarantee that the things that you'll learn will give you more pleasure than actually hooking and landing a fish.

INLETS

Inlets are narrow passageways of water between two points of land. These narrow openings are usually located on a barrier island and act as major transitory routes for all marine species which seek food or shelter in our back bays. Early in the spring a major migratory movement gets under way as many baitfish enter our bays to seek nourishment and to procreate in protected waters. On their tails are schools of gamefish, stripers, blues and weakfish, some of which have already spawned and others which are looking to do so in the bay. Since the narrow inlets often act as the only outlet for bay water to drain into the ocean, strong currents

Rips that form over shallow, rocky reefs can be counted on to produce fish in daytime as well as nighttime.

develop along the inlet shores. Many inlets also feature rock piles or jetties along their banks. These have been built to stabilize the fragile underwater sand structure within the inlet and prevent inlet boat channels from becoming too shallow. When you take into account the large variety of marine species that populate these jetties, the presence of deep water in close proximity to the shore, the strong currents that sweep in and out of the inlets and the fact that they serve as a major thoroughfare for baitfish to enter and exit the back bays, you can understand why these areas receive more attention from surfcasters than any other location. Many of these areas have parking within close proximity to the water. These spots attract crowds and space is often at a premium when fishing along the banks of an inlet.

One of the more attractive features of fishing inlets is that regardless of the weather conditions, the confines of the inlet are almost always fishable, even in a raging Nor'easter. Like most other locations in where we seek fish from the shore, inlets are much more productive during the hours between dusk and dawn than they are in the daytime. Boating traffic through the inlets coupled with the reluctance of gamefish to come close to shore under sunny skies, makes for some poor fishing during the day. This does change somewhat in the fall as gamefish become more aggressive before their migration southward but even then nighttime often holds the key to better fishing. The backsides of the inlets are preferred by those who like to employ light tackle and can be a very productive places to toss small plastic swimming plugs and bucktails while the actual mouth of the inlets are usually fished primarily with heavier bucktails, darters and deep diving metal lip swimmers. In the late summer, baitfish leave their protective surrounding of back bays and start to congregate on the backsides of inlets. Some years, baitfish can be so thick that this is actually a hindrance as it is hard to attract a gamefish to our lure with so much bait around. However, as sure as the sun will rise over the eastern horizon tomorrow these massive congregations of baitfish will depart these areas at some point in early fall and surfcasters anticipate this event with glee as it usually signals the start of the fall run. Tide and currents have an exceptionally strong influence here on the availability of bait and consequently on the presence of predatory gamefish. Although is hard to make general statements regarding which tide period is more productive in the inlets, the time tested strategy is to fish these waters on a dropping tide. As the water recedes in the back bays the small baitfish have to abandon their hiding spots in the eel grass or along the marsh banks and retreat into deeper waters. Once they do that they often find themselves at the mercy of currents which can sweep them toward the mouth of the inlets. As this massive body of water makes its way towards the inlet, a bottle neck effect occurs as too much water is trying to fit in the narrow opening of the inlet. This in turn creates strong currents along the length of the inlet. On its own merits this alone might be attractive to gamefish but what makes it even more appealing is the tendency of the current to wrap itself around inlet structures and create unstable, fast water rips. These types of areas are by far the most heavily fished by surfcasters within the inlet and there is a very good reason for that. When I fish the inlets I will often jump from one rip to another and don't even bother wetting a line in places in between, that's how much importance I place on these areas. Let's take a little deeper look into what exactly makes these areas remarkably productive.

RIPS

Rips are created when the natural flow of water is impeded or obstructed by some kind of structure, natural or man made. It can also be classified as a stretch of turbulent water caused by one current running into or across another. For a surfcaster, these rips present possibly the best place to wet a line as they attract more attention from gamefish than any other beach structure. We can find these rips anywhere where current strength is sufficiently strong to force water around or over some type of structure. Without the benefit of the current, for example around jetties on the open beaches, there is not enough pressure being built up along the side of the jetty in order to create a rip at its tip. Most productive rips are found either within the confines of inlets or other narrow openings in the land where great amounts of water are squeezed through a narrow area or along open beaches where currents are strong. These fast, unstable waters serve as hunting grounds for stripers and bluefish as they are able to navigate these rips with ease while the smaller baitfish struggle to swim in them. In order for them to form, many rips require a strong water flow and many do not form until the tide has been dropping or rising for a few hours. They also last for a limited time during each tide period and then dissipate as the current eases. The surfcaster has to be familiar with the structure he is targeting in order to present his lure under the most favorable conditions. He also has to learn at which stage of the tide the rip will form, how long it will last, at what depth the fish will be positioned and where exactly, within the confines of the rip, will they be stationed. He has to be familiar with the effects of the moon tides as they increase the current strength, particularly around the inlets and he also has to have an understanding of how certain winds will effect the formation of a rip. For example, an "in your face" wind will probably move the rip closer to you while an "over the shoulder" wind will most likely move it away. After he gets familiar with these things, then he can start thinking about which lure might be most productive. Each rip is generally more productive on one stage of the tide. Whether it is the incoming or outgoing mostly depends on the type of structure that is causing the rip to form. Let's use as an example an inlet jetty that has a deep hole on the east side. On incoming water the ocean is pushing a lot of water through the narrow inlet opening, creating a pressure along the jetty's west side until it rounds the tip. Here at the tip it blows off but immediately falls into the hole on the tip's east side. In addition the current coming from the ocean is now colliding with the current that is traveling along the jetty and the water starts to swirl, creating a very turbulent rip. On the backside of the rip an "eddy" or a "backwash" forms. The "seam", an area where the rip ends and the backwash begins can be one of the most productive parts of the rip. Fish will often rest in this backwash which features little or no current and patrol the edges of the rip. Holding a large subsurface metal lip wobbling along this seam is my favorite way to fish these rips. In addition casting in front of the rip and letting a darter or a bucktail swim through the rip on a retrieve is also a deadly strategy. Don't overlook the west side of the jetty either as current will be building up pressure there too, sweeping baitfish from the sandy beach and pushing them along the rocks toward the tip. Conversely, on the outgoing tide, the water builds up along the eastern side of the jetty but once it clears the tip the swirling effects of a rip are not nearly as pronounced because the bottom is flat and unobstructed at the point were it meets the current coming straight out of the inlet. For this reason, I usually concentrate on incoming current here instead of outgoing. This is just one example of a rip that I like to fish and am familiar with but each rip has its own characteristics, nuances and the only way to get proficient at picking the fish out of it is to spend time at your favorite hole and note the changes in the rip's formation during different stages of tide, moon periods and wind direction. Although inlet rips are among the most productive places to fish, they also present a never ending educational experience. Changes to the bottom structure, frequent bouts with weedy conditions around new and full moons, constant changes of current speed hour by hour and even the occasional disappearance on the part of the gamefish when we think they will be there can be absolutely maddening. Don't fool yourself, deciphering these deep water rips are not as simple as figuring how and when they will form. Consideration must be

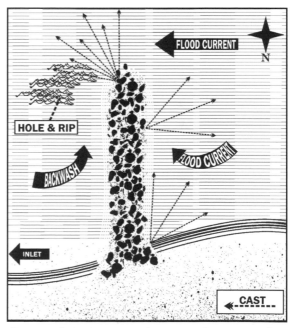

Casting along the jetty in the areas where current has meaningful impact is often the difference between success or failure.

also given to time of the year, which baitfish is the primary food source for the gamefish and of course which color or lure profile might be the "right" one. That's what makes it much more satisfying. When you put all your knowledge together about tide, current, moon and wind, it can pay off in a big way.

For a beginner the easiest and simplest approach to fishing these areas is to use bucktails primarily until one gets a feel for the area. I would start working bucktails as close to the bottom as possible without dragging sand or snagging on rocks. You will most likely have to increase the weight of a bucktail as the current picks up in speed or decrease its weight as the current weakens. Although I use deep diving metal lips in these area a lot, especially ones fitted with eel skins, I still consider the bucktail to be the most productive and versatile lure to use in these deep, fast waters. Don't be afraid to think outside the box in these spots as those who are willing to stray from conventional thinking are often rewarded for their efforts. Quite a few years ago, I fished a jetty rip with a friend and although we had adult bunker jumping clear out of the water in front of us, we were drawing blanks casting bucktails, metal lips and darters. In desperation, I tossed one of those gigantic plastic shads up-tide and retrieved it slowly through the rip in vain. After few casts, I tossed it back into my bag which was lying on the rocks. My buddy asked if he could use it. "Knock yourself out," I told him as I sat down on a large boulder to take a breather. I watched him struggle with that six ounce lure. His rod was bent like a pretzel and seemed ready to explode under the pressure of the cast. Somehow he managed to lob the darn thing but instead of up tide it ended up on the opposite side in the backwash. He was now reeling the big shad against the current, a cardinal sin I thought to myself as I chuckled under my breath. The smile froze on my face in an instant as his rod doubled over under the strain of a large fish. I quickly jumped up and slid down the rocks to help land his fish. After weighing it, I released a mid-thirty pound class striper. I found myself in a bit of a pickle as I did not realize that getting back up would not be quite as easy as sliding down moss covered rocks. I attempted to do an awkward crawl on my belly when my friend shouted "Stay there, I got another coming to you." Ok, now I was getting annoyed. After releasing his second fish, I found my way back to the top, just in time to catch his cast going towards the backwash instead of up tide. It was bad enough he had three fish in the thirties that night while I failed to elicit a bump but he did it by casting down tide and retrieving against the current. On the way back I asked why in the world he would even consider working a lure against the current. His response was bunker often face into the current and since we had bunker in the rip the presentation that we gave to the fish "wasn't right". In addition he shared with me his theory that resident blackfish and sea bass will face into the current when venturing outside the protection of the boulders." Don't forget" he said "they are predators too and are looking for food in the current ".I learned an important lesson that night, never take any part of the rip for granted.

ROCKY SHALLOW RIPS

Rip formation on the open beaches is usually a storm related occurrence. If a strong wind is prolonged in duration from the same direction and especially if it's blowing diagonally onto the beach, a sweep is created. This sweep can act similar to a current when it encounters a structure in its path, creating turbulent water around it. Because of high winds that usually accompany these storms, we often are forced to use heavy bucktails, tins or bottle plugs to cut through the wind with our cast. Once the winds have abated, the rips disappear and the water around these structures moves at a much slower speed. There are other types of rips which don't really fall under either the inlet or open beach category. The best example would be the rips that form around the north side of the Montauk Point Lighthouse. Strong currents develop here as Long Island Sound is looking for an outlet to the ocean on a dropping tide. Squeezed in the nar-

Rocky points can often be very rewarding places to cast a lure. Deep water in close proximity and the tendency of these points to alter water flow are equally attractive to the surfcaster as they are to striped bass.

row area between Block Island and Montauk Point the current races along the shoreline, sweeping the baitfish with it. Eventually it reaches a series of shallow rocky reefs on the north side of the lighthouse. A series of rips develop over these shallow areas but the plugs that are productive here greatly differ from the ones I use in the inlet rips. Because of the shallowness of these structures, darters and needlefish are top producers at night while pencil poppers, especially Gibbs Canal specials and my favorite, large Yo-Zuri Surface Cruisers, do a lot of damage in the daytime. Bucktails do produce here too but on a dropping tide, the surfcaster is often forced to wade far onto the reef in order to reach the fish which are also retreating with the tide. You must use a bucktail heavy enough to reach the fish but light enough so that it does not hang up on the rocks in this shallow water.

ROCKY BEACHES

Probably the most productive structure along our shoreline is found on rocky, boulder strewn beaches. Sacred grounds like the beaches of Block Island, Montauk Point, Cuttyhunk or Rhode Island are made out of boulder fields and are considered by many to be the most consistent fishing grounds for a surf fisherman on the east coast. This is not surprising, considering that stripers have earned the nickname "rockfish" because of their preference for these rocky areas as their hunting grounds. Unfortunately these rocky beaches are also the most difficult places to fish and some surfcasters never quite make the transition from the sandy beaches to these rocky areas. Let's face it; these spots are not for everyone and besides, being a rock hopper does not give you any more ability or knowledge than fishing on the sand. Standing on slippery boulders in pitch darkness as the angry ocean is doing its best to knock you off your perch is an acquired taste, especially when you add to the equation the difficulty of landing a fish under these circumstances. The promise of great fishing is however too much of a temptation for me and it overpowers any fears I might have about fishing this unfriendly terrain. In addition, these rocky shores put an extraordinary amount of pressure on our gear and tackle. Constantly trying to keep a fish from heading to the next boulder in order to free itself, reeling with our equipment submerged at times, crawling over barnacle covered rocks or just trying to stay dry after being swept off the rocks every few casts, requires an angler to keep his equipment in top shape. Inferior tackle quickly shows its warts under duress. Having said all this, I still have not found a more magical place to wet a line than standing in the darkness of the new moon, perched on a large boulder on Montauk's south side, casting metal lips in the white foam and expecting the fish of my dreams to smack it at any moment. All these rocky areas, although different from each other in some aspects, from current speeds to water depth, do share some similar characteristics. First, the abundance of resident baitfish and crustaceans which call these rocks, boulders and kelp beds their home. Second, the striper's preference to have some type of structure which they can use to hide their presence and to create ambush opportunities when they are feeding. Remember, these fish posses the ability to make short and powerful bursts of speed during the attack and

Fishing amongst the boulders in the darkness is one of the best ways to capture that fish of your dreams.

they need structure in order to maximize their skills. Large boulders provide resting places around which stripers can take ambush positions yet still be out of the current or rough water. Even at the peak of the nastiest storm, when water is churned up into a froth, one side of any rock will take the brunt of the punishment while the opposite side will provide tranquility. Why? Because the front of the rock will serve in a gale just as it does in the fast inlet rip. It will divert water around itself leaving a much more tranquil backwash on its backside. Can you guess where our friend the striper will be positioned? Right on the backside of that rock, conserving its energy and yet ready to pounce on anything that the sea brings its way. Why is the striper's position important, particularly on these rocky beaches? If we know its location or we are at least operating under the assumption that we know where the fish might be laying it is easier for us to make a correct presentation around that boulder with our lure. I always prefer to present my lure in a way so that my lure will benefit from whatever water movement I am confronted with. This usually means casting up tide and let the lure drift towards the boulder as any baitfish would if it did not know there was a striper waiting behind it. If I am targeting a specific boulder I do not expect a strike to occur a few feet from it or right in front of it. Neither do I expect anything to happen once the lure has drifted far away from the boulder. I might be operating within narrow guidelines but I find that most stripers will not stray too far from their ambush spot to chase the lure so if I am targeting a specific structure, in this case a boulder, you bet I'll do my best to present that lure within inches of where I think the fish might be. Of course, when fish are active and cruising around, this all changes but I find that this attention to detail is important early in the year when stripers are not heavily feeding and in particular in the daytime when fish might get wary of feeding under the bright sun. By retrieving our plugs tight to the structure and in the same direction the water is moving, our success rate expands exponentially compared to just blind casting in all directions. When it comes to the choice of lures to use in rocky areas, as with any other place, this depends on many variables. Current speed, water depth and wind direction are some of the more important things to consider. The presence of baitfish and its availability also deserves consideration. If I had to generalize I would say darters, needlefish and metal lips at night with pencil poppers and metal lips during the day. I don't particularly care if the water is deep or shallow in order for me to use bucktails. My preferred water for these lures has very little to do with depth and all to do with type of water movement. If this rocky area features a reef and there is ever-present white water rolling off it or if a particular beach has a good current flow the bucktail might be the most productive lure. You must work it slowly enough to just stay off the rocks. If the rocky beach in your neck of the woods features calm, still water, find another beach. The beaches without any surf to bring it to life or no current to replenish it with baitfish and nutrients are lousy places to fish. Granted, if I had to, I would most likely try fan casting needlefish when there was no white water or current. I would not expect fish to be stationed at any particular location in such structure but instead scattered through the area looking for food. Walking and casting, as much as I don't like this technique, might be the best way to run into a school of cruising fish.

BACK BAYS, HARBORS AND ESTUARIES

Fishing in these areas bears very little resemblance to ocean front beaches. Long rods are replaced by smaller, lighter sticks. Standing waist deep in the water is often unnecessary and a lot of fishing here is done by actually standing on the banks or marshes with your boots completely dry. The large lures are also replaced by a smaller, 3 to 5 inch Bombers, Rebels and Redfins, small paddle tails and of course, bucktails. In the spring, these are the areas which get populated by migrating stripers first. Look for shallow mud flats that will warm up in the early spring sun on a dropping tide. Once the tide changes direction the warm mud will warm up the incoming water and stripers will become more active. Small lures work well early in the year and they have to be retrieved at a very slow pace as these fish are not that aggressive in the very cold water. Most of these fish are schoolies and since they will have to be released anyway why not crush the barbs on your hooks to aid in the release. As the season progresses and adult bunker move into many of these areas, you'll generally begin to find some quality fish. Those dunking chunks have an advan-

Peanut bunker are often on the menu of harbor blues in the summer months.

Fishing with light tackle along the back bay marshes can be a very rewarding experience especially if you are looking to tangle with weakfish.

tage over plug casters but a pencil popper worked at the edges of the bunker schools in the early morning or large metal lips retrieved at night in the same manner have fooled many cows. As the spring progresses sand eels and spearing receive most of the attention from gamefish and bucktails with thin pork rind and tins fitted with tubes are probably the most effective lures. Teasers fished ahead of the lure work well in these calmer waters all year particularly when fish are zeroing in on worms or grass shrimp which are difficult to replicate with wood or plastic lures. The marshland's drainage ditches and little creeks become especially productive from here on as small baitfish find protection here from predators during high water. These small bait fish must retreat out of these shallow areas as the tide drops. Fishing the mouth of these locations with small swimming plugs and bucktails has always been a sure path to success. In back bays marshlands look for drop-offs close to the shore and work your lures close along the drop. You will usually find gamefish feeding along the edges of the drop-off during time of moving water. In the summer I like to take advantage of a pattern that develops in the harbors as big schools of bluefish feast on peanut bunker. Storm shads and pencil poppers work best but I have to warn you this can become an expensive proposition and you might go through quite a few plastic shads. Late summer finds snappers or baby bluefish creating havoc with the local spearing population. A lot of surface commotion and silver flashing takes place which serves as an attractant to stripers who move in to investigate. Believe it on not, large blues move in too and will readily gobble up their young. Chrome pencil poppers are probably the most effective lure for stripers and blues and if you want to go after the snappers themselves, a small Kastmaster will do the trick. This by the way is a wonderful way to introduce kids into the surf as snappers are usually plentiful and generally easy to catch. Many of these areas serve as a nursery for juvenile baitfish and juvenile gamefish during the year and this abundance of life never fails to attract predators. Although larger fish might be present in these shallow areas, they usually seek comfort and safety in the deeper holes in the bays or harbors during daytime hours. Fishing during the night often holds the key to getting a shot at bigger fish. Many of these areas are very shallow and fish do not have a cover of white water as they do on ocean beaches. A stealthy approach is a must, with minimal use of lights. Slowly wading instead of sloshing through the water is required as even loud chatter can put the fish down. Small 4 to 5 inch Scandinavian type swimmers are by far the most productive lures especially when used in conjunction with a teaser. Once fall arrives, these areas can perk up as baitfish and gamefish start leaving these waters for their migration southward. Nighttime is still better than daytime as far as consistency of fishing is concerned with dawn holding an edge over dusk. Keep in mind, these shallow areas get a lot of boat traffic during the day and it usually takes a few hours after night fall until the gamefish feel safe enough to come into the shallows. This should be taken into the account when planning your excursion in these areas.

BRIDGES

All the fish in these protected waters are not small but the truly large fish are usually found resting in deeper holes and only accessible to boating anglers. In my opinion, the best chance of tangling with a big fish in these calm waters is in the fall around local area bridges. The lighting on these bridges attracts massive numbers of baitfish which are migrating and making their way towards the mouths of the inlets. If large bait like adult bunker is present you can be certain that some large bass will be taking residence in the shadows of the bridge, ambushing them as they are carried with the current. Obviously it would be difficult to generalize what time or tide would be most conducive for this type of fishing as each bridge and its banks usually feature numerous rips, drop-offs and flats which might be productive on different stages of the tide. For my money, I would place my bet on outgoing current after midnight when boats are safely tied at the docks and most other surfcasters are in their beds. Fishing around these types of structures might be the most unforgiving terrain you will encounter fishing from the shore as large fish will often head straight for the bridge abutments if caught in close proximity of the bridge. For this reason light rods have no place here as stiff rods and strong lines are needed in order to prevent large fish from wrapping you around barnacle encrusted posts. In late November, when a lot of surfcasters have stowed away their gear as the nights become cold and frost is nibbling at your finger tips, some of the best fishing takes place under the lights of the bridge. Large baitfish like herring and shad move in through the inlets and populate the bays, giving surfcasters a last chance to land the fish of their dreams. Because these baitfish are large in size they often attract the truly big cows and I have often watched these magnificent creatures lined up like cordwood in the shadows from on top of the bridge. I don't however fish from the top under any circumstance and therefore it would be just plain wrong to give you advice as what strategies to employ. Although I know what takes place on these bridges and how one should proceed when fishing them, I never was comfortable with the release methods employed by those who fish here. I usually fish on the banks adjacent to the bridge by swimming subsurface metal lips, bucktails or rubber shads in the shadow lines that the lights on the bridge create. Some nights you can almost time your hits as the lure is working from the lighted area and

Casting from the banks adjacent to a bridge and letting the lure drift into the shadows created by the bridge lighting can produce fantastic results especially during fall months.

enters the shadow lines of the bridge. The fish will often be waiting in the darkened area or behind abutments darting into the current and ambushing the bait before retrieving to their original positions. As the current increases the metal lip become less productive unless you move away from the bridge giving you longer time to get them deep. Bucktails and large shads however really come into their own during strong current flow as they can get down deep in a hurry where fish are usually holding.

CHAPTER SIX

— STRATEGIES —

There are many things that go through the minds of surfcasters as they get themselves ready to make their first cast. All of the factors that will contribute to the failure or success of the outing include but are not limited to water temperature, wind direction, tide phase, current direction and speed, moon phase, the presence of baitfish, the choice and color of the plug and even the visibility of their leaders under water.

One thing that in my mind should be of the foremost concern of a surfrat but receives very little attention is presentation of the lure itself. We get so caught up in having the latest bunker patterns and fish scale finishes that for some reason we start thinking that fish will just commit suicide as soon as they see our latest and greatest lure. Granted, the brains of fish are very tiny and am I not insinuating that they posses enough intelligence to refuse a good offering. But then again, we have all had our plugs ignored at one time or another because the fish were obviously zoning in on something we did not have in our plug bag. However, I do believe that fish intelligence is developed enough to tell the difference between a good and bad presentation of a lure.

For example, a lure that is cast down current and retrieved against the current will rarely receive attention from gamefish. Consider the fact that gamefish are usually set up on the downside of structure. This means that our lure is retrieved right over their heads yet they show no interest in it. How come? The answer is simple, because the lure is moving unnaturally in the wrong direction against the current! Honestly, when was the last time you've seen a baitfish going the wrong way in an inlet? It just doesn't happen that often. With this in mind, the presentation of a lure becomes very important.

Now that we have dealt with the direction a lure should be presented, we can now deal with the proper retrieval speed. If what we are trying to accomplish with our lure is to imitate a baitfish that is struggling in the water, then this is the reason why most sharpies advocate the slowest possible retrieve speeds. We are trying to imitate an injured baitfish and I've never seen a struggling baitfish zoom through the water at high speed. This is the primary reason for keeping our presentation on the slow side. Most lures that are retrieved even slightly faster than they are designed for will also lose most if not all of their action and effectiveness. Darters will just zoom through the water instead of zig zaging, while bucktails will fly through the rip and poppers will skim the surface.

This brings us to the most important part of a correct presentation, the preference of fish to ambush bait instead of chasing it down the beach. It is well documented that fish only feed to sustain themselves and therefore will not expend more energy feeding than they will gain by the calories consumed, calories out versus calories in. This means anything that zooms by at high speed gets automatically ignored, particularly by stripers. Bluefish will on occasion give chase to a fast moving plug but I still find a slower presentation more effective as it generates more hookups.

As the fast pursuit down the beach is out of the question that leads us to the usual feeding behavior, feeding through ambush. Think in terms of a police officer patrolling the highway. If he has to chase every driver that drives over the speed limit for miles to give him a ticket he'd be out of gas quickly. But if he takes an ambush position in the bushes, along the highway, and then only needs to zoom after the cars for a short distance before retreating back to his original position, his tank of gas will last a lot longer. Not just that but he can issue more tickets in the same amount of time it would take him to complete just one long distance car chase. Fish feed in the same manner, they do not set up around the structure to engage in a playful chase with bait. They are there for one reason and one reason only, to eat as much as possible in the shortest amount of time while wasting the least amount on energy doing it.

MATCH THE HATCH: DOES IT WORK?

Most surf fishing strategies evolve with time; some are quickly forgotten while others having more staying power. However, they all share a common trait; they are all dependent on the type of baitfish that is most prevalent in our waters. Over the years we have gone through the mackerel craze where you just had to have a mackerel patterned plug. The fish obsession began when swarms of large sand eels inundated Cape Cod and Block Island, not to mention the "golden" years when juvenile weakfish were so prevalent in the surf that gold over yellow plugs were all the surfcaster wanted.

However, these things come and go but one tested strategy has stood the test of time. The most likely reason is that it is not dependent on a particular color but rather the size of the lure. "Match the hatch" is as prevalent today as it was in the early years of the sport. For those who have yet to come across this popular phrase, it is best described as a method of trying to match our lure to the baitfish that the game fish are feeding on, at that particular time of the season. In the spring this means long, slender lures that are supposed to imitate

Matching the hatch to the most predominant bait in the surf is time honored tradition among surfcasters.

sand eels. In the fall we increase the size and profile of our lures to better match larger baitfish like bunker and herring. During the mullet run "blue" patterned plugs are all the rage. The new "peanut" type plugs that are supposed to imitate peanut bunker are the "in" lures of the moment for targeting game fish feeding on these oily baitfish . When you first think about it, this seems like a "can't go wrong" strategy and to some extent the notion is correct. Yes, blue plugs take their share of fish during the mullet run but then again most of the plugs tossed have blue on them. How can any other color stand a chance? I've done just as well with yellow or white lures during mullet runs, besides, if you are using a surface plug half of its body (and most of the "blue" part) is sticking out of the water. I'd argue that in this case the "color" is less important than the choice of a lure. Going "over the top" and fishing the top water column with surface swimming metal lips and poppers is what will get you strikes as bass and blues have their sight fixed upwards towards the surface where the mullet are congregated. Throw a bucktail or even a chunk and watch your success and confidence plummet while everyone is into fish on top water lures. But I digress, if only because of my inability (exasperation might be a better term) to come to grips with "color" as being most important when choosing a lure. Presentation, in my mind, is the most important consideration when tossing a lure in the surf. After all, if your lure appears to the fish like a piece of wood or plastic, what difference does it matter what color it is painted?

WHITE BAIT LUNACY

Many of us have been fortunate to experience daytime blitzes that occur on the rocky shoreline around Montauk Point in the fall. Acres of striped bass and bluefish can be observed in each rising wave gorging on "white bait" (bay anchovy). Clouds of these tiny baitfish often swarm around the rocks we stand on and we can only imagine the massive amounts of them that must be present further out in the deeper water. Having this massive amount of bait and game fish present within a rod's length of an angler should equate to a day to remember for those lucky enough to be present at the time. Not necessarily!

Frankly, sometimes these "blitz" conditions will result in the most frustrating days a surfcaster will experience during a season. How can that be? Plentiful bait and game fish on their tails cannot ever be considered a bad occurrence. Isn't that right? It can happen when fish are "zoned" in on one plentiful bait and just slashing through the schools with open mouths. Often the fish will ignore every lure thrown at them including painstakingly tied fly fishing creations. There is just too much bait for the fish to be interested in our lures, and that creates a problem. There are very few things more frustrating for the surfcaster than casting into the middle of blitzing fish and not getting a bump. All year long we cast into what is seemingly an ocean devoid of life, picking a fish here or there while concentrating on night tides. Now you are standing in the water with fish up to your armpits and they refuse to touch any lure you toss at them. How can it get more frustrating than that? Yet when you think about it, it makes sense. Why do we expect our lure, which matches the hatch exac ly, to be noticed when there are thousands of little baitfish that look just like our offering swimming around our lure?

I believe "match the hatch" terminology was coined not by surfcasters but by fresh water fly fishermen. In crystal clear, shallow streams wary trout are not easily fooled by any contraption an angler might come up with. Catching trout requires a presentation that almost exactly matches the insects floating in the stream. Fly fisherman painstakingly tie their flies to look like and behave like the bugs that are hatching at the moment. What they don't have to contend with is a tightly packed, massive school of baitfish swimming in a confined area. Do you really think that if there was a massive amount of insects floating in the stream, the trout would take the fisherman's fly rather than the real thing? Probably not, just as your "peanut" plug might be ignored when you toss it into a school of peanut bunker on the ocean beach.

EARLY BETTER THAN LATE ....

I find that the "match the hatch" approach works better early in the year when baitfish are scarce and predators are focusing on a single baitfish instead of just going through schools of bait with their mouths open like whales. Once the baitfish schools become large and dense, the "match the hatch" approach, in my opinion, loses its effectiveness. In fact, during the fall run it can become a hindrance to one's success. Tossing a lure that looks like a million other baitfish and hoping that it will get singled out by a predator is more akin to a "Hail Mary" pass at the end of a football game. Toss it out and hope it sticks…to something. More times than not it will be your treble in the back of a baitfish instead of the predator you seek.

One example is fishing when spearing are the predominant bait. They often gather in large schools, tightly packed and in close proximity to the shoreline. You'd have to admit that a teaser ahead of your lure, regardless how expertly it was tied will have a hard time standing out among all that bait and enticing a gamefish to strike. But work a large Bomber or a medium to large sub-surface metal lip and watch spearing depart on both sides of the plug, creating a large hole and consequently making your

When presented with a lot of small bait in the area go "loud and large" with big pencil poppers or metal lip swimmers.

plug a focal point of the scenery below the surface. This will often initiate a strike. The same bass and blues which showed very little interest in chasing after spearing can often be enticed into striking by presenting a larger meal. Consequently, those who usually do best in the Montauk white bait blitzes do it with lures that show little resemblance to the actual baitfish stripers are feeding on. Medium to large metal lips with white single bucktail hooks in the tail cast into the foam left by a cresting wave will often produce a strike when nothing else will. Here, the foamy white water provides a few precious moments in which the angler actually has an upper hand when it comes to the presentation of his lure. Before the foam dissipates, your metal lip will now be seized by the striper, which can sense the movement on the surface in the foam, even though it can't see it clearly. They will reflexively strike it almost immediately. Once the foam dissipates, the fish can see your plug clearly and will usually refuse to hit it.

Another downside to hatch matching is the fact that most of the baitfish in our area, with the exception of adult bunker, are of the small variety. Late in the fall, shad and herring usually, or I should say hopefully, bring some quality bass in the surf zone but most of the year we are presented with the steady presence of spearing, small sand eels and peanut bunker. If you downsize your offering you should expect to catch smaller, more aggressive fish. The fact is that large fish will seldom, on a regular basis at least, come charging after small baitfish. Why would you then expect that cow bass will strike your small lure? Throw a large metal lip, eel skin plug or a rigged eel and you should expect to cull the biggest fish present in that particular area at the time.

Matching the hatch is a great concept when bait fish are n~~
fish are feeding aggressively. However, for most situations I wou~~
it as a starting point in my trip. If I find immediate success, fine, I'll stick
with it, but if I need to make modifications in the size of my offering, I will
only go to larger lures. Smaller ones might get me more fish but bigger
lures are the only way to go if you are looking for a good bend in your
rod and a peeling drag. Next time you are presented with large concen-
trations of bait and fussy fish, try going with a "large and loud" approach.
Big metal lips or ruckus causing pencil poppers are often the only way to
induce a strike when too much bait is present.

As you can see I am not a big fan of the "match the hatch" routine. I
believe that lures in the range of 5 to 7 inches are just dandy for most situations. They will not turn off the small fish as monstrous 8 inch metal lips
might, but they provide a large enough profile for big fish to find appealing. I also refuse to believe that fish will pass on a larger meal in order to
feed on tiny baitfish. There are exceptions however and they have more to
do with the location an angler is fishing in than the actual lure size or
shape. For larger lures to work amongst smaller bait you will need either
of two things, a strong current which will leave fish a limited time to decide
if it wants to take a swipe at your lure before it swings out of the strike
zone or white water to "mask" the presentation of the lure. In my opinion
darters, needlefish and metal lips all excel under those conditions.
However, I doubt you will find them as productive in protected backbay
waters.

This brings me to another point. Where are all these tiny baits usually
located that we have to toss these tiny lures in order to catch a fish? Not
on the ocean front usually but in sheltered waters of harbors and back
bays. I have had many unfortunate instances when I had to fish during
either a worm hatch or when tiny grass shrimp were capturing the attention of game fish. Let me tell you, it is not pretty. As hard as I have tried to
"match the hatch" with jelly worms, teasers or plastic shrimp while stripers
were sucking in everything in sight all around my feet, I usually have had
little success in drawing a strike. If you have ever seen either one of these
occurrences, I think you'll agree that the numbers of these creatures in the
water is staggering. Our teaser looks like just one out of a billion of those
tiny creatures floating along in the current. If you were a betting man,

what would it take for you to accept a one in a billion odds to catch a fish? I would rather stay in bed than take those odds. I feel that most of the reason for downsizing the lure under these conditions is because the baitfish and the fish are of the smaller variety. A seven inch plug might scare more fish than it will attract. As I said before, I think matching the hatch will work much better when bait is dispersed and not heavily feeding. I do however believe that matching a color scheme to the most prevalent bait is a better idea than matching it in size. My thinking applies strictly to subsurface lures and I feel that if the fish are zoning in on a particular baitfish they will usually prefer a color that closely resembles that species. I know many will disagree with me on this but I really do feel that too much is made out of the "match the hatch" strategy and if you are to follow it to the extreme you might end up frustrated with mostly small fish.

Working the beach structure be it a boulder, rock pile, sandy point, bowl or a cut in the sandbar is often the key to a successful night in the surf. Walking and blindly casting along the beach is a good exercise routine but not much more than that.

WORKING THE BEACH OR WORKING THE STRUCTURE?

One of the strategies employed by many surfcasters today is the "walk and cast" routine. By using this strategy a surfcaster walks the beach and fan casts in all directions before moving down the beach and repeating the process. It is said that by using this approach a surfcaster can cover a lot of water. I would ask exactly what kind of water are we talking about? Is the water fishy, highly oxygenated, fast moving water or desolate, unproductive and fishless? I would say the second one is what you will encounter most of the time. I don't know about you but I put a very high value on my time. At home I have a wonderful wife and two great kids and sometimes it pains me to leave them. The call of the surf however is too strong to ignore and I find myself often wondering if I ever will reach that nirvana-like state in my life when I can fish and be with my family at the same time. Until then my time is limited and in my mind, it has to be justified.

When I make my plans for a trip to the beach my first consideration is what structure am I targeting and what is its appeal. Is it the right tide or the right wind? Is it a report from friends about yesterday's action or is it just a feeling that I have about that particular piece of real estate? Whatever the deciding factor is, once I get there I am not going to leave this carefully planned trip so I can "fan cast" along the beach. If you take time painstakingly to pick a particular structure where you think the fish might be congregating, why in the world would you walk away from it? You say that particular location wasn't productive. Fine, get in the truck and go to another one! Don't walk the beach hoping you will walk into the blitz because that almost never happens.

Imagine two hunters finding an oasis with water in the middle of the desert. They take positions in the tall grass knowing that animals will come here to drink at some point during the day or night. After a short time one hunter declares he will go "walk and hunt" through the sandy desert. How many animals do you think he will encounter in the middle of the desert? Probably as many as will be encountered using the fan casting technique on an open beach. My point is, work the structure that you have confidence will hold fish. Your thought process on selecting a final destination does not have to resemble one of a Nobel laureate but you do have to think more in terms of a hunter, taking all things into consideration including tide, wind, bait and structure itself in order to give yourself an edge. Otherwise you are just hoping the fish will be there.

If you know from prior experience that fish like to congregate in certain locations during certain winds, then those are good reasons to go there. If you saw large bait present on the backside of the inlet today and you feel they will get flushed out with the outgoing tide in the morning that is even a better reason to go there. Working the beach and blindly casting, hoping, praying that something in that vast ocean takes pity on your lure is not a good strategy. Becoming confident in the structure that you are fishing does take time. Numerous trips will have to be logged under different conditions in order to find a pattern of when and why gamefish are feeding there. Once you learn the spot and its tendencies you will not only acquire the knowledge that comes with it but confidence too. Those who have confidence in a location and have a game plan, will work structure from different angles with different lures at different depths. They know that although beaches extend themselves as far as the eyes can see, only a few locations can be counted upon to hold fish. Those who don't have confidence in the spots they are fishing or are lacking a well thought out plan walk and cast, and usually end up with sore feet.

DAY VERSUS NIGHT

There comes a time in the life of every new surfcaster when they will start questioning their success rate in the surf. They might hear about great

catches by others which will intrigue them and make them wonder why their catches are not comparable. Regardless of which route they might take to educate and improve their skills, such as reading a book, joining a club or just asking questions on internet fishing message boards it will all eventually end up pointing in the same direction, the need to fish after dark.

Seeing fish crushing top water lures in daytime is pleasure for the eyes but the hours of darkness are often the key when targeting larger fish.

I have always been fascinated by the transformation that takes place in our ocean once the sun sets over the western horizon. The hordes of swimmers and sun worshipers vacate our beaches which in the becomes strictly the domain of the surfcaster. Most pleasure have been crisscrossing the ocean in search of a few fish all day ly tied to their docks. The beaches which appeared bare a few hours ago began to teem with life as gamefish move into shallow water under the cover of darkness to look for food. In my opinion, regardless if you're able to buy all the fancy equipment, the best lures and drive the fanciest beach buggy, none of that will help you increase your success rate more than if you just start to fish primarily at night. In the fall when the bait and game-fish migration takes place you will get a chance to find some consistency in the surf during the daytime hours but even then the nighttime action will generally be more productive than daytime. During the nighttime hours the noise level is reduced, the swimmers and boaters have departed and gamefish feel safe enough to come in from the ocean or deep holes in the bays to cruise around structure looking for a meal. With this in mind we should also keep our noise level to a minimum. Shouting and yelling is often counterproductive especially in calmer waters found on the inside of our inlets. The use of lights should also be kept to a minimum as they can spook fish rather quickly. Wading on the flats should be embarked upon with the determination of a snail, slow and steady without sloshing through the water. The most important aspect of fishing at night might have to do more with our psyche than with anything we actually do. The fish are often very, very close to the beach. So close that you could often touch them with your rod if you knew they were there. This is very difficult for most surfcasters to accept as they continue to work deep water with long casts. I like to make a cast from the dry sand before I ever enter the water and have been often rewarded with fish that were just cruising in the small drop that is created from waves constantly pounding the lip of the beach. When retrieving a lure, finish your presentation at your boots particularly on sandy beaches for the above reason. Many times fish will follow our plugs all the way to the lip of the beach and lunge at it at the last possible moment as it suddenly realizes that it is running out of room and your lure might escape.

On the jetties I like to retrieve my lure until it hits the base of the jetty below where I am standing. Yes, my plugs get pretty banged up by doing this but I find that more fish are cruising along the edge of the jetty than they are at the end of my cast. Think about it, these fish came to the jetty looking for invertebrates, small fish and crustaceans that live in and around the jetty. What purpose would it serve to cruise 30 yards away from the jetty and away from this smorgasbord?

Keep your retrieve at night as slow as possible as gamefish are rarely attracted to speedy presentations during these hours. Most importantly, learn to trust your lures .Knowing what your lure is doing under water or on top of the water and being able to picture this in your mind will go a long way toward making the right presentation to the structure you are targeting. If you are confused by hundreds of color patterns and are not sure which one works better at night versus the day you can do two things. You can use the strategy that is often repeated in surfcasting circles by going with dark plugs on dark nights and lighter plugs on bright nights. Or you can do what I do and fill your bag with yellow, white and black plugs and concentrate on your presentation instead of worrying if you have the hot color in your bag. Either way, regardless whether you got started in surf fishing yesterday or ten years ago, concentrating on the night tides will improve your success rate and most likely the size of the fish you catch. If you are not comfortable in the dark of the night or you just can't fit it into your schedule, try concentrating your efforts in the early morning hours or during cloudy, overcast days. Both of these periods are much more productive than fishing under the bright sun. At dawn, when darkness gives way to light, baitfish are often disoriented by the changing light conditions and this is something gamefish exploit remarkably well and can often be found feeding heavily for a short period before retreating to deeper water. Overcast days also result in reduced visibility in the water which emboldens stripers and blues to move into shallow waters, looking for food.

UNCONVENTIONAL STRATEGIES

You might wonder why a discussion of "unconventional strategies" is included in this book when there are so many strategies that have been time tested through the years. The primary reason is that in surf fishing nothing is constant. The structure you absolutely love might disappear after a single storm, bait might vacate the area during a single tide and fish will sometime ignore the same lure they crushed just yesterday with abandon.

Unconventional strategies are not something you should get
they don't work often enough in order to be utilized on a regula,
they will save you many a night of anguish when the water arc
seems devoid of life or even worse, when there are many fish around but
you can't get a touch. Believe it or not, there are quite a few of these
unconventional strategies to chose from. In a way these techniques are
only limited to the size of your imagination. What I am saying is that you
should not box yourself into thinking that you must do what everyone else
is doing especially if the fishing is slow. Think outside of the box, throw a
tin at night, explore a little by using different retrieves and speeds. The
point of this sport in my opinion is to catch fish and not to be uniform or
look good doing it.

This brings me to strategy number one, the one that is responsible for
more raised eyebrows than any other, using poppers at night. Pencil poppers can be effec-
tive in the dark but
your best bet is to
concentrate on
nights around
the full moon
when the sky is
bright. I like to
work my pencil
popper even slow-
er than in the day-
time with frequent
pauses during the
retrieve. Letting a
plug rest complete-
ly for a few sec-
onds before resum-
ing the retrieve can
at times induce a

Try "swimming" a Super Strike 2 & 3/8 ounce sinking Little Neck popper at night by using just a simple straight retrieve. Keeping the lure inches under the surface accounts for many fish landed each year.

strike from a fish that has been drawn in the vicinity by the thrashing of a
pencil popper. I do have to say that I find this technique better on ocean
front beaches and fast moving rips than I do in the calmer water in the

back bays. There in the shallow, placid waters you might do more damage by causing a ruckus on the surface that might literally spook any fish that finds itself in the vicinity.

At night I prefer to use standard poppers instead of pencil poppers but not in the way you might assume. Sinking poppers, particularly the Super Strike Little Neck 2 & 3/8 ounce are deadly when retrieved just under the surface with just a straight retrieve. The elongated neck on this plug gives this lure a little swimming motion, not a lot but enough to be very effective. In addition, because of its great casting ability it makes a wonderful way to deliver a teaser over the sand bar. I find these lures to also be most productive on sand beaches, particularly when there are nice, clean sets of white water coming over the sand bar.

When using a darter or a tin, after your cast and when the lure hits the water, initiate a retrieve similar to what you would do with a pencil popper. Vigorously shake the rod tip while keeping your retrieve to a bare minimum for a few seconds and then resume a regular retrieve. This action often will entice a gamefish to investigate the commotion and then it will attack the lure when you start your regular retrieve. You can accomplish something very similar with metal lips by "sloshing' your plug through the water after a cast. After the plug lands give your rod a quick, strong jerk and then let the plug rest. This works great on sandy and rocky beaches when the water is calm and fish are not aggressively feeding as they often do when white water is present.

Another technique you might consider trying is to work a slim needlefish on the surface like a pencil popper during the day. In early spring when fish are often zoning in on thin, long baits like sand eels a skinny needlefish worked over the top can often illicit more strikes because of its profile than standard pencil poppers. When working the inlet rips and you have plenty of elbow room, try casting your darter or a diving metal lip swimmer and letting out a hundred yards of line out until the plug reaches the end of the rip before you start a slow retrieve. Many times the big fish will be positioned far away from where your plug lands and away from the strong currents around the shoreline and this is the only way to get them on your hook without buying a boat.

As you can probably notice, most of these techniques are not that strange; there is a reason why they are productive. If you utilize them occasionally, particularly when you are not catching fish they might give you the confidence to use them on those slow nights that will come your way. Trust me; this sport is not easy even though we are dealing with fish that have very tiny brains. The failure rate is ridiculously high, you are dealing with unpredictable species and you are also at the mercy of the whims of Mother Nature. Adding another weapon to your arsenal of knowledge might just be better than shoving another pretty lure in your already overstuffed bag. There are times when it pays to be unconventional!

CHAPTER SEVEN

— BAITFISH PROFILES —

I struggled mightily with this chapter for reasons you might find a little unusual. At first I considered dedicating the whole chapter to "color", its selection, my preferences, urban legends and old wives tales. The more I thought about it, the more I was bothered about writing about stuff I don't believe in. I could have written a few pages based on popular theories, told you to fish dark lures on dark nights and light ones on moon lit nights. This advice is prevalent today in the surf fishing community as well as in print and on the Internet. The problem is I don't believe in any of that and I feel I would do a disservice to you, the reader and myself if I wrote about the stuff I consider suspect at best. I know it is hard to swallow that all your questions regarding which color to buy won't be answered especially when you consider just how many pretty patterns there are on the market today. But I have always felt that presentation and not the color of the lure is the main ingredient a surfcaster needs to concentrate on in order to find success in the suds. Yes, I am very well aware of some "must have" patterns", like the need to have a blue lure during the mullet run. The problem with this particular pattern is that most of the guys fishing the beach have heard it and will not toss anything but blue plugs. How can we gauge the efficacy of another color if everyone is tossing the same darn thing. I'll let you in on a little secret; white works just as well as blue does during the mullet run.

What is more important is how you present your lure. Where in the water column and how you retrieve it. These are the factors that will spell the difference between a few fish or so many that your arms will hurt. Since mullet travel on the surface, stripers will be zoning in on the top of the water column. I would bet good money that if you threw the bluest of the blue lures you have but your lure swam close to the bottom you would go home fishless. How can I be so confident? On numerous occasions I have seen bait slingers throw the freshest piece of bunker into the school of feeding stripers during the mullet run and then wait for a strike... that never came. Stripers that are chasing mullet clear out of the water ignored the bunker chunk not because they weren't hungry but because they were concentrating on what was going on at the surface, in other words they were looking up not down.

It's the same thing with lure color. You can have the prettiest lure on the beach, painted in a pattern so close to the real baitfish that it is hard to tell them apart. But if you present this lure improperly you have almost no chance of hooking up. With that in mind I decided that a profile on the baitfish that frequent our area would be more appropriate and hence this chapter. Against this background it will become more obvious to you what lure you should select when a particular baitfish is around and what retrieve should be used. To me this is far better than repeating some old wives tale about which colors work and when. After all, if baitfish prevalence is not the primary influence on which color we use, then I don't know what is!

An experienced surfcaster knows that during the season there are a variety of baitfish migrations, with baitfish moving from the surf zone to the back bays and from the back bays to the ocean front. One baitfish will come and another might depart and some might stick around the whole season. The key is to understand how different baitfish affect the feeding habits of the game fish we pursue. Although game fish have to eat, they do not necessarily do it in the same manner on a day to day basis. I hope that by profiling baitfish and game fish feeding tendencies, It will help you in your lure and color selection when planning a trip. That is the purpose of this chapter.

PRETTY PLUGS

Before I start let me make a confession. I am a plugoholic. I own more lures than I care to admit and I just hope that if I pass away suddenly my wife won't sell them for what I told her I paid for them. I own them in every shape, style and yes, dozens of different colors. Why do I own so many different patterns when I believe that color is not an important part of choosing a lure? The answer is simple, paranoia. Fear that one day some lure will be hot and I won't have any. That is the only reason why I have so many.

I fish mainly three basic colors: white, black and a lot of yellow. I find that fish very rarely refuse to hit my plug because it's not the right "color." It does

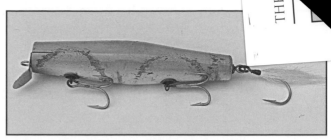

Fancy lures look great in a display case but plugs with a lot of "mojo" like this Danny are often the first lure I pull out of my bag.

happen but not often enough for me to carry three dozen lures in my bag. I've been on the receiving end of some serious spankings over the years but also I have dished it out on more than one occasion, by having success with certain colors. Still, I always start my trip with a yellow plug and work through my colors from there. I find that yellow has the most visibility under water and therefore becomes easily noticed by gamefish. If it's daytime I might go from yellow to white or another light color. At night I will try a black plug if the yellow fails to elicit strikes. I am so confident in my approach that I might go against the grain sometimes and toss a completely different color just to see if it's the color or the presentation that is actually catching fish. It drives my friends nuts! Presentation of a lure to the structure is what gets results. After all, do you think if a lure is presented correctly the fish will say: "No thanks, its not my color?". I doubt it. The only thing I find more important than presentation is confidence in the lure you are using. Unfortunately, confidence is not something you can read about or buy in a tackle shop. You need to experience and harness it because it will change your whole outlook on how you fish. More on confidence in an upcoming chapter. For now, let's get back to our baitfish profiles.

BUNKER

Bunker, also known as menhaden or pogy in some parts of the northeast are one of the most important baitfish species that take up residence in our waters. Not only are they a rich source of protein for the gamefish but they are also filter feeders that eat plankton and keep our bay waters clean. According to research the adult bunker can filter up to four gallons of water a minute through its gills. How incredible is that! They can grow up to a pound or more and because of their size and their oily make-up

Big bass feeding on adult bunker has resulted in some remarkable action on New Jersey jetties in recent years.

and high caloric content they are a very desirable baitfish to have in the area. Why? The main reason is that they attract large fish. Bunker congregate and travel in large schools, so big that some have been measured to be over 40 miles long. In the bays or the surf they are usually identifiable by their "flipping" routine as they frequently flop about on the water's surface. This activity is part of their natural behavior and it's not necessarily a sign that predators are in the area. Their tendency to flip however gives a surfcaster a very good idea as to which lures to use in order to imitate this behavior. Since bunker spend the majority of their time close to the surface, this supports the notion that surface lures are the best in emulating their behavior. Pencil poppers and to a smaller degree other standard poppers are tops in daytime. In addition, large metal lip swimmers "sloshed" through the water intermittently during the retrieve are also a great presentation during the night. Keep in mind that stripers in particular like to circle the schools of bunker looking for a single baitfish that appears most vulnerable. An injured bunker will eventually end up at the edge of the school as it doesn't have the strength or mobility to keep up with the healthy specimens. With this in mind always work your pencil popper or metal lip at the edge of a bunker school instead of casting into the middle.

For those times when bunker are not showing or they are under the surface in deep current, a big plastic Storm Wild Eye or a Gibbs 3 ounce Casting swimmer (bottle plug) are very good choices. Bunker bodies are very oily and are known for their rapid deterioration after their demise. Sometimes it is possible to see an "oil slick" on the surface of the water or a strong stench might fill the air, usually signs of bunker getting crushed by bluefish under the surface.

There are many color variations today in regards to what exactly is the "right" plug pattern to emulate bunker, particularly among lure builders. I have an approach that some have called simplistic but I find that it works for me, so I am sticking to it. I prefer a slightly greenish to yellowish top and a pearl belly when I am targeting waters laden with bunker. However, please understand that with some plugs such as pencil poppers or metal lip swimmers a significant portion of the plug is out of the water. Therefore, I doubt color makes that much of a difference. The only color I always insist on when I use bottle plugs is yellow. The reason for this choice is that the entire plug is beneath the surface and therefore visible to the fish. If color is an important factor then this is the time when it should be. Your principle strategy should be to concentrate on using plugs that work the top of the water column and that have an erratic motion imitating bunker. This is more important than pulling your hair out trying to pick a color that you think the fish want.

MULLET

The importance of mullet as a food source for stripers and blues is really not that evident in the surf during the spring and summer. In late summer this changes in dramatic fashion as they start to congregate on the backsides of inlets in preparation for their fall migration. Usually after the first September cold front and consequent temperature drop, the mullet vacate the confines of the back bays and head southwest along open beaches. Traveling in tightly packed pods they attract a lot of attention from gamefish. They are easily identifiable by the "V" wake they leave as they swim just under the surface. Unlike bunker, that often travel in deep water once they clear the confines of an inlet, mullet are usually found in the troughs between the sand bars and the beach. Quite often they are found very close to the lip of the beach where the sand meets the water. Long casts are often unnecessary as gamefish will shadow the pods of mullet into shallow waters. As mullet swim on the surface game fish will also focus on the surface activity and working a subsurface lure is usually very ineffective during these times. Metal lip swimmers and popping plugs are absolutely deadly when mullet are in the wash, especially when cast almost parallel to the shore. You want your plug to spend as much time as possible in the area where mullet are present and since they are traveling tight to the beach, diagonal casting gives your lure more time to work in the most productive area.

Mullet always travel east to west and north to south. As a result it is not necessary to chase a single pod of fish down the beach as another pod is probably coming along the beach in a few moments. What is important is to take a position on a beach where some type of structure will become an obstacle to the mullet and slow their westerly or southerly movement. This will keep the mullet in one place for a period of time and afford you of the opportunity of having them in front of you for a while. I have often observed pods of mullet navigating through the trough undisturbed until they reach that part of the beach where they encounter some type or structure, whether it is a jetty, sand bar or point. It might be a shoal or they might get pinned in between two jetties or better yet, when they have to cross over a shallow turbulent sandbar.

One of my favorite types of structure is a sandbar that runs parallel to the shore and then turns towards the beach. At the point where the bar meets the beach, turbulence is created by waves running over the shallow bar. Even if there is less than a foot or two of water, stripers will often setup in this area and feed voraciously. For them it is a veritable mullet "buffet" being delivered into their mouths. The mullet that have traveled in the deep trough unmolested up to this point, now find themselves tossed in the white water as they try to cross over the turbulent waters on the bar. On many occasions a surfcaster who is positioned on this structure and is tossing metal lips into the foam will outfish everyone tossing popping plugs, by a large margin.

A few years ago on a fall day, four of us worked this type of structure during the mullet run. There was a stiff onshore breeze creating nice white water where the bar met the beach. However, we decided to fish the deep hole just in front of the bar as we had seen mullet splashing in the trough. We started casting blue poppers almost in unison but soon found nothing but frustration. The frantic movement of the pod of mullet, breaking the water in panic, made it evident that game fish were in the area but we found no takers. I walked away and decided to try the shallow sandbar twenty yards away. As I attached my metal lip swimmer to my snap I wondered exactly how far I was going to be able to cast it into the stiff wind. I found out almost immediately as the wind knocked my Danny swimmer down during the first cast. If my plug traveled thirty yards that was a lot, however on this day it did not matter as my plug immediately disappeared under the surface as it hit the water. I could see striper tails trashing on the surface while their heads must off been rubbing in the sand. On each consecutive cast I landed a fish! That proved to be too much for my friends who joined me but soon found out that poppers weren't what the stripers wanted. All the action was taking place in the first thirty yards of the beach. We landed twenty two stripers that day; nineteen were caught on a metal lip swimmer while the other three came on popping plugs. Needless to say, no matter how stiff the wind was none of those guys was ever going to show up again without a metal lip swimmer during the mullet run.

HERRING

Very few things excite surfcasters, in the northeast, more than the presence of adult herring in the surf. In the spring, anticipation builds among the surf crowd as they wait for herring to make an appearance in the estuaries and bay areas. Herring are an anadromous species that spend the bulk of their lives in salt water but return to freshwater to spawn. In this

Changing light conditions during early dawn hours often trigger gamefish to go on a short feeding binge.

regard they are similar to striped bass. In late fall they make a return appearance and are usually responsible for some of the best fishing of the year. This usually occurs in November and but recently it has been taking place in December so take this into consideration when you are debating if you should hang up your gear early in the season.

There are over 200 recognized species of herring swimming around the globe and they all share a similar characteristic, a protruding lower jaw and lack of lateral lines. The juvenile herring feeds on plant plankton by filtering water as its passes through its gills. The adult herring feeds on tiny ocean plankton and small fish. The attraction of having herring in the surf has a lot to do with its size as Atlantic herring can grow up to a foot and a half in length and can weigh over one pound. Baitfish this size, often attract big stripers from the deep water rips and if it is not too late in the season you can bet that gorilla bluefish will not be too far away either. The most popular color pattern used in emulating herring has remained the same for many decades. Light blue top, pink sides and white belly is considered a gold standard among all lure builders although you will find a slight variation in the shade of blue or pink from builder to builder. Herring spend most of the daytime hours in the deeper water venturing to the surface to feed usually only during darkness. When they are present along the ocean front however subsurface and surface lures are equally effective. My favorites are large pencil poppers and extra large Danny and Atom 40 type metal lip swimmers during the day with large six inch or bigger rubber paddle tails at night. If the weather is snotty or you are fishing a place where current is strong, you cannot beat a large bottle plug or a large darter.

SAND EELS

The family name for the sand lance, more commonly called sand eel, is "Ammodytes." This means "sand burrower" which relates to their tendency to bury themselves in the sand to avoid predators and strong currents. They prefer cooler water temperatures than most of other baitfish that are found in our area. They can be found in the surf or the bays in early spring and then again later in the year. In northern regions where water temperatures are cooler, sand eels can be found year round, even in the summer months. They travel in dense schools and move similar to eels by twisting their bodies but they are not related to real eels. The have elongated thin bodies and it is this characteristic that has a lot of influence on which lures are most effective when they are the primary baitfish in a game fish's diet.

In my opinion, long and slender tins like the A007, A17 , Charlie Graves sand eel imitators or Point Jude PoJee and Sand Eel lures, dressed with a green tube or a single bucktail hook are the best choice for imitating the shape and behavior of sand eels. As sand eels love to dig into sand, a tin can be dragged over the sandy bottom with intermittent jerks to create a "puffing" effect on the sand. This action can fool a game fish into thinking a sand eel has just come out of hiding. Bucktails with elongated hair profiles and dressed with slim pork rind have also always been excellent producers when sand eels are around. This is also true for Slug-Go's and Fin-S plastic baits. Taking into consideration where sand eels are found in the water column, bucktails, tins and lead heads should be worked in the bottom half of the water column for best results.

Needlefish lures with their slim profiles are also very effective especially when used in conjunction with a Red Gil teaser. Red Gils are very popular plastic baits that are a dead ringer for real sand eels and they have accounted for some fantastic catches over the years. In addition, small plastic minnows like Bombers or Rebels can also be very effective in the calmer waters of back bays or estuaries. When it comes to color selection, tan seems to be the pattern most often used by sharpies. However, when trying to look like the real thing I have often done well if not better with lures that have a greenish back, silvery sides and a pearly belly. Then again, I've done just as well with yellow needlefish. Presentation and profile is in my opinion what you have to be concerned with. The color pattern should be the third thing on your check list.

SPEARING OR SILVERSIDES

Spearing or silversides are the most common baitfish in our local waters. The benefit of spearing for a surfcaster lies not only in their numbers but the fact that they spend most of their life within a few feet from the shore line. In winter they seek deeper waters to avoid extreme cold temperatures. Most surfcasters were probably exposed to this long thin

Stripers are often feeding on small baits in the spring which requires light rods and small lures in order to make a good presentation.

baitfish as children, when using them as bait for either snappers or summer flounder. They are one of the primary food sources for striped bass and bluefish in the bays during the spring and summer months. Most of the feeding by bass and blues takes place at night under the cover of darkness. Stripers in particular are fond of just sucking spearing and often times you will hear slurping noises on the surface as a striper gulps water along with the spearing. Unfortunately, this type of feeding and the fact that these baitfish are plentiful often makes presentation difficult. The hits will often feel like bumps as a striper sucks in and spits out the plug immediately. Green and olive colored plastic minnows such as Bombers or Hellcats are usually the best imitation, especially when used in conjunction with a thin profile teaser.

It can often be a frustrating experience when spearing are around as you can clearly see that fish are present and feeding but it's hard to elicit a solid hit. What works sometimes is experimenting with different retrieve speeds until you find something that works. In daytime the spearing and the predators that are feeding on them are not as concentrated as during the night time, but good action can still be found if the concentration of spearing is large enough to attract the predators. On open beaches, tins with a single bucktail hook, like Point Jude Po Joe lure, can be effective in particular when used in conjunction with a teaser. In August spearing become a major food source for snappers, or young of the year bluefish. The commotion snappers create, as they chase spearing, draws attention from game fish. That is why small pencil poppers account for a lot of fish during these times, especially in the calm waters of back bays and Long Island Sound beaches and harbors.

BAY ANCHOVY

Certain locations get massive influxes of this small baitfish, also called "white bait or rain bait." In the fall, Montauk Point has benefited greatly from their presence for the last decade. Millions if not billions of these tiny baitfish can be found in late September through early October swarming around the boulders and rocks at Montauk. At times they can be so thick an angler has to wade through them to get to his favorite rock. When fish find them they tend to seek protection in numbers by tightening up in small shoals. When herded into confined areas the bass and blues mercilessly slash through them. Most of this action occurs in less than a few feet of water around and even behind protruding rocks that surfcasters are standing on.

Small metal lips up to 5 inches fitted with a single white bucktail hook and small bucktails with thin pork rind can be deadly. A hundred or more stripers per day, per angler is not that unusual an occurrence when the anchovies arrive. In fact, this is one of the rare occasions when daytime fishing will out produce the night tides. Unfortunately, there are also times when this bait is so thick that stripers ignore everything thrown at them. Throwing casting eggs or floating poppers (as they are called in some locals) with saltwater flies are just marginally productive and so are the teasers. Both of these are just slightly better than other plugs. The only thing that works sometimes is a large pencil popper worked at the edges or beyond the feeding school of stripers. The commotion it generates on the surface stirs the competitive juices of the feeding bass and blues and they will elicit savage strikes. Mostly it is not uncommon to retrieve your plug by bouncing it on the backs of hundreds of stripers and not elicit a single hit. The downside to this massive bait presence and daylight feeding frenzy is that night action usually suffers because the fish have been binging all day. Once this baitfish disappears the daytime action usually slows down but the night time fishing generally can be counted on to pick up.

SQUID

"Squid hound" is one of the many nicknames that striped bass have earned over the years, since fishermen have always thought that they love to feed on squid. Strangely enough research in recent years has shown that very few bass actually had squid in their bellies. You would think that squid would be one of the primary food sources for stripers but research has shown otherwise. Very few of all stripers examined in one study had either squid or eels in their belly. In fact, the most common food source in their intestinal tract was crabs. This might be the reason a friend of mine who experienced great fishing in the early 80's commented to me recently: "We use to catch linebackers, short and thick. All we get now are the receivers, long and thin." Regardless of their recent feeding habits what is important for a surfcaster is that stripers absolutely love lures that imitate squid and they will rarely pass the opportunity to crush one. Darters that move in a zigzag fashion similar to squid, particularly those dressed with a long feather or a bucktail on the back hook, are deadly when squid are around. A large eye on the back of the plug might be very desirable as squid have eyes larger than any other species of similar size. Pink, red, burgundy or any other shade of red is a primary color when trying to imitate squid. Since squid change their colors to camouflage their presence and blend into their surroundings, the actual color reflects whatever terrain they might be swimming in so don't work yourself up into a tizzy trying to come up with an exact imitation. Keep in mind that their bellies are a lighter color than their backs, which also helps disguising their presence from prey and predators. Other lures that work well at this time are needlefish dressed with a rear bucktail hook, bottle plugs and of course bucktails. Regardless of which lure you use, keep in mind that if the squid is what you are trying to emulate, you

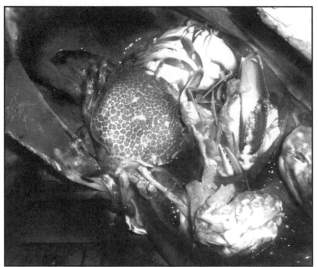

Although the presence of bait is a prerequisite for blitz conditions most of the time you'll find bass grubbing the bottom in search of crabs and sand fleas. No wonder crabs are the food source most often found in the belly of a striper. What unearths these crabs and sand fleas when they burrow themselves in the sand, exposing them to voracious appetite of prowling stripers? White water turbulence, of course.

should make your lure move in an irregular fashion, imitating squid which move in short bursts of speed.

JUVENILE WEAKFISH

There was a time when hordes of juvenile weakfish would inundate the surf zone in the fall and paint the water gold. It is one of the explanations why yellow darters have attained an almost cult-like following around Montauk Point. This was the place where we used to see most of these young-of-the-year weakfish, as they were migrating out of Peconic Bay and along its shore, until they made a turn southward and seaward. Unfortunately, weakfish numbers have been on the decline for many years now and it is very rare these days to see their young in any numbers along the beach. It does happen occasionally however. One fall I was socializing at the Gathering of the Anglers in the Montauk Point parking lot when I received a cell phone call that juvenile weakfish were beaching themselves west of Jones Inlet trying to escape predators. As inconspicuously as possible I slipped out of the parking lot and gunned my truck towards Jones Inlet. Within an hour and a half I was in the water casting gold poppers that gorilla bluefish and some quality bass were crushing on the surface. The entire surf line, as far as one could see, was littered with juvenile weakfish that were flipping on dry sand trying to escape the sharp teeth of big bluefish. Gold and yellow popping plugs and metal lip swimmers worked great in the daytime and the same color darters and large bottle plugs at night

LARGE WIDE BODY BAITFISH

When I hop onto a jetty I often find myself instinctively looking for a rip that might be present at the tip, hoping that any small bait in the area will get swept into the rip. What I sometimes fail to take into consideration is how many species call these rock piles their home. Big fish the likes of bergal, sea bass and blackfish live year round amongst the rock crevices and are considered to be one of the most desired meals on a striper's menu. Unfortunately for stripers these fish don't venture too far from the rocks during the time the current is strong and therefore avoid being swept through the rips. Once the current wanes they do leave their protective surroundings to look for food but still stay in close proximity to the rocks. With this in mind, presentations of our lures should be as close to the rocks as possible and if possible parallel to the jetty or rock pile. Expect hits to be vicious in nature as gamefish are well aware that they have no room for error as blackfish will head for the safety of the rocks as soon they detect the presence of a predator.

Large shad bodies like the ones made by Storm or Tsunami are very effective in mimicking the size, shape and profile of these fish and the wobbling paddle tail makes them appear alive. Large subsurface metal lips the likes of the Tattoo Diving swimmers or Beachmaster Cowboys are also deadly especially when fitted with eel skins. Their agonizingly slow rate of retrieve and a wobbling motion can entice even the most wary gamefish to take a swipe. Since these fish spend most of their lives amongst the rocks their bodies almost reflect the color of their surroundings, helping them camouflage their presence. With that in mind I go with a dark patterned lure, black and pearl, black with gold sides and even all black.

LARGE SLENDER BODY BAITFISH

Occasionally we get graced with the presence of large slender body baitfish like tinker mackerel, kingfish, needlefish, garfish and eels. Unfortunately this does not happen that often which is too bad considering that large baitfish usually attract some very large stripers. Large, needlefish like Super Strike and Beachmaster Wads or Hab's 9 inch model are by far the best imitations of needlefish and eels. In addition, slim body darters like the ones made by Super Strike and Gibbs are very effective when tinker mackerel are the predominant bait. If the mackerel are of the large variety I'd put my money on a Gibbs 3 ounce bottle plug in mackerel pattern and work it in the sweep or strong rip.

CHAPTER EIGHT

— MIND OVER MATTER —

One often over-looked part of fishing is the mental state of the fisherman, in particular, the level of confidence they have with their techniques and the lures they are using. Many of us are bombarded with advice on color, shapes and size of the lures every place we turn. From popular fishing web-sites to seminars or our friends, it seems like everyone has an opinion about what works, where and why. Yet bring up "confidence" and they will sheepishly tell you that they have one, maybe two lures they feel confident enough to fish with their eyes closed.

In order to hook and land a giant bluefish like this one you will need confidence in your lure and your equipment.

Considering we have no visual contact with most lures we use, it becomes of utmost importance for an angler to "know" what his lure is doing under the surface by the vibrations telegraphed over his line to his rod. Anglers need to feel confident that their bucktail is floating in the right part of the cresting wave or that their deep diving metal lip is reaching the depths that it is designed for. This is a game of inches; there is no such thing as a "good enough" retrieve or even a good enough cast. Yes, you might get some success without obsessing over what your lure is doing but I can assure you that you will always leave the beach feeling a sense of inadequacy because someone spanked you badly. Take it from me, I've been there.

You got into the sport because you were intrigued with fishing. Now you are reading this book because you, like the rest of us, want to know more about this sport we love. Take the next step and become one with your lure. Don't just cast it out and hope that something sticks to it. Imagine your lure as it swims through the water and soon you will get a sense of exactly when and where during your retrieve a fish will find it. The confidence one has in the lures we use cannot be bought, bartered or sold, it must be earned. It takes many nights of wasted sleep and futile casts to get to the point where you trust your lure enough that you can relax and gaze at the stars during your retrieve. But once you have got it, you'll have it for life. The best part is you will be able to take a similar lure from any other builder and in a few casts figure out its strengths and weaknesses and adjust your presentation accordingly. Without confidence you'll probably aimlessly search through your bag for a "hot" color, one that will save your night. But hot colors are here today, gone tomorrow. However, the confidence in your lure will stay with you forever.

HOW AL GOT HIS CONFIDENCE...

A few years ago I had the pleasure of fishing with my friend Al on the north side of Montauk Point. As we got into the water in the darkness every rod around us was bent under the strain of a fish. I knew from experience that most of these guys were tossing darters so I attached one to my line and told Al to do the same. Two cranks of the reel handle were all it took for my rod to bend under the weight of a fish, just like everyone else. Everyone but Al. While the rest of us were bailing fish on every cast he struggled with his retrieve. Finally he walked over and said "I can't feel it working." That was strange considering the current was ripping over the shallow reef. I told him to just relax, cast up tide and retrieve just fast enough to stay in contact with his plug. The excitement of all those fish trashing around him got the better of him and now his casts started sailing every which way but up tide. He retrieved the darter so fast it started to skip over the surface. This went on for a good half an hour until he declared that he was done and walked out of the water. The rest of us were still up to our armpits in stripers but I figured I had enough fish to take a break. The problem is, in Montauk, if you walk out of the water there will be another guy on your rock when you get back in the water. As I debated what to do, I could see Al's flashlight going on and off as he was rum-maged through the back of his buggy. As he began walking towards me, I hoped he changed his mind about quitting. When I saw he was still in his waders I was relieved. At this point the fish had moved in closer and our darters were only getting smacked close to the shoreline. However, on some casts the darters would get buried in the rocks before the fish got a chance to get to them. Al walked back into the water and cast a small bucktail. Now, I knew that guy was a bucktailer extraordinaire but I was not prepared for the spanking I was about to receive. Regardless of what I used, even bucktails of the same size, darters, or needles he was out-fish-ing me now five to one with a darn bucktail. It got to the point where it became Al's show while the rest of us watched. He was so confident in that bucktail that his confidence was oozing out of him, he felt every rock his bucktail came in contact with, every piece of kelp that was swaying in the current and it was almost as if his bucktail had eyes and was guided over the boulders while the rest of us were getting helplessly hung up.

At the end of the night I told him: "I want you to become as confident with the darter as you are with that bucktail." What I didn't tell him was that I secretly wanted to have his level of confidence using bucktails. After that night we did not fish together for a few years until we met again last fall in Camp Hero. I was on my way to scale down the soaring cliffs at Camp Hero and into Browns where I was planning to toss some bucktails in the juicy white water, my newest obsession at the time. He was just getting up from sleep in back of his truck. Tired and groggy he told me he had a bunch of fish on the north side last night. I knew last night

Large stripers often charge the beach during periods of inclement weather.

was a bust from other guys who had fished there. In fact, I gave up at midnight myself without a bump. There was a rumor though of one guy's flashlight constantly going on and off but no one knew who it was. Then Al blurted out, "I had so many fish last night I should have just left my light on. It was actually a pain in the butt turning it on and off every few minutes." Then he added "I killed them on darters! Black, white, yellow, it didn't matter. As long as I stuck my index finger in front of the reel and let the line slap during the retrieve, I had fish".

I walked away content knowing Al found what he was looking for in his darter. A few minutes later as I unhooked yet another striper from my rock at Browns I looked at my bucktail and I knew I found mine. We both attained enough confidence in our lures over the years that it changed the way we fished. Once you gain confidence in your lure you will cease to rummage through your bag every few casts looking for a hot lure. The "magic lure" is not in your bag, it's attached to your leader. Learn how to use it and you'll realize that any lure is only as good as the angler that is using it.

INTUITION

Webster's dictionary describes intuition this way: "The power or faculty of attaining to direct knowledge or cognition without evident rational thought and inference." Huh? I always thought of intuition as something I used as a reason to beg my wife to let me get out for the umpteenth night in a row. Conversations usually start like this: "Honey, I got this feeling that fish will be at the inlet tonight." She'll usually go on to remind me of my past "intuitions" that turned into disasters. "But wait a minute, what about all those that turned out to be gold ", I say. Seriously, though, I think intuition is an important part of a surfcaster's psychological preparedness. Acting on your intuition might not be as silly as it might seem. After all, there is a reason why your intuition kicks in. It's usually based on something you experienced in the past or something that you didn't participate in but know for sure to be true.

Here is an example. A nor'easter is barreling up the coast. You know by listening to the weather reports that tomorrow morning the winds will be 30+MPH out of the NE and sheets of rain will be coming at you horizontally. The high tide is at 10 a.m. That means you have a few hours to pack your stuff, call in dead and head for Montauk's north side first thing in the morning. You intuition is telling you to park yourself under the Bluffs and toss big bucktails into huge swells coming over the lighthouse reef. But you don't. Instead you stand on the subway train with your fellow strap hangers, trying to read your paper while the guy next to you is snoring

and the lady in front of him is clipping her nails. Now your phone starts to ring but you don't know it because the city subways have no cell phone coverage. Finally you drag your rain soaked body to your office, collapse in your chair and check your voice mail messages. You can't tell who it is exactly that is yelling a message, but he obviously is standing outside as you can hear the strong whistling sound of the wind. All you can decipher is "get your butt out here, 30's and 40's

Good things happen to those who follow their intuitions.

are all over the beach." You check the phone to see who exactly called you then you remember you talked to your best friend last night and shared your intuition. He followed your intuition and you didn't. This has happened to me so many times in the past that I had to promise myself that if I can act on it, I will. Intuitive thoughts do not happen without reason, they are subconscious messages from King Neptune asking you to come and play. Learn to trust them and they will put you onto more fish than reading Internet or newspaper fishing reports.

CHAPTER NINE

— DARTERS —

From a historical perspective the lure designs manufactured by the Creek Chub Lure Company are much more significant than most surfcasters realize. Although their lures were designed with freshwater anglers in mind, it did not take long before saltwater anglers realized that their large models used for fish like musky were well suited for use in the surf. Surfsters, darters and pikies were just some of the lures freshwater anglers had at their disposal since the beginning of the century. In the early 1950's, Massachusetts master plug builder, the late Stan Gibbs, designed a lure that had a darting action when used in water with a strong current. According to the legend, Stan perfected the design on the beaches of Montauk Point along with the late Johnny Kronuch, the owner of Johnny's Bait and Tackle in Montauk. Today's surfcasters have a dizzying array of needlefish, metal lip swimmers, poppers and pencil poppers to choose from but when it comes to darters the selection is drastically limited. Part of the reason is that darters have a well deserved reputation of being the most difficult lure to build out of wood. It seems that it is very difficult to get the same swimming action in all the plugs, due to the differences in density of the wood. One might question that statement considering how simplistic in form these lures appear to the naked eye. However, the truth is there has never been a more "temperamental" lure made that anglers use to cast into the surf. Most of the other lures can still be effective if a through-wire is slightly off or the hook hole is a quarter inch off of where it should be. Not darters! If the slope on its head is off by a few degrees, the lure will be unbalanced and won't swim correctly. In addition, if the through wire protrudes slightly off center the lure becomes nothing more than a hunk of wood that rolls on its side. Most garage based lure builders follow tradition and make their darters un-weighted out of rock maple which is hard on tools and builder's hands. I can tell you that every time the people who make Beachmaster lures decide to make a batch of darters, I get phone calls from them every day in which they both swear they will never make them again. Every few years however they eventually give in to the demands of their customers. But, take it from one who knows, they hate every minute of making them.

Fortunately, we have two manufacturers that don't use rock maple in their process to build darters, Gibbs and Super Strike. You can purchase these lures and be assured that they will perform as advertised. Their most popular models are what are described as "slim" darters .Gibbs made them the old fashioned way out of pine wood, while Super Strike darters are made out of plastic. Gibbs has recently come out with a wide body 3 ounce darter that runs deeper than their slimmer version. Tattoo's Tackle has recently joined the fray with their own 3 ounce model and Beachmaster Lures makes batches based on the late Danny Pinchney designs.

The wide body darters run much deeper than slim darters and are particularly effective in pulling fish out of deep water rips around jetties or inlet channels. Due to their large profile they are especially effective when big profile baitfish like herring, shad or bunker are prevalent and the primary bait source for stripers. Unfortunately, their deep diving characteristics also make them a very poor choice for use along open sandy beaches without much of a falling slope. This type of beach makes the water generally too shallow for these plugs to work prop-

Darters are most productive in waters that feature ample current movement.

erly. Slim darters are much more versatile as they can be used in just about any location where gamefish like to gather. Of course casting a shallow running darter in a deep rip will greatly reduce your chance of hooking up as very few fish will rise up from the deep to take the offering. So choose your weapon carefully.

Regardless of their shape, thickness or size all darters share one common characteristic, they all move in a zigzag pattern. Some will begin their action within a few feet of line retrieval, moving to one side and then the other and back again, repeating the movements every few feet. Other darters have a more irregular and unpredictable movement. To me, they imitate two things very well, one an injured baitfish that often swims on its side and two, a squid which likes to dart when it feels threatened. In order for a darter to work properly it must be used in current driven waters. They are deadly around breach ways and inlets, river estuaries or any point that extends into the surf zone. These structures and locations impede the natural movement of water and as a result generate currents and rips. It is these currents and rips that add to the action of a darter and entice predators to attack the lure. There is no better example of this than Montauk Point which extends 120 miles into the Atlantic Ocean, east of New York City. On a dropping tide the waters of the Long Island Sound come flowing out towards the Atlantic Ocean and around Montauk Point. As a result a large amount of water is leaving the Sound and is compressed between the boundaries of Block Island and Montauk Point. Thus, this large and rapid flow of water creates wonderful currents and rips close to the shores on the north side of Montauk Point. This fast moving water is also often diverted onto the shallow rocky bars, reefs and deep holes around the Point where rips are also formed. Baitfish are pressed along the surf line as they seek refuge from the swirling water where they can be ambushed by predators. Stripers and bluefish, as well as other predators, are no strangers to this behavior and they set up in these spots waiting for the current to deliver easy meals. The strong swimming ability of bass and blues enables them to navigate the turbulent waters with ease unlike the smaller baitfish which are often helplessly carried and tossed about by the strong currents and rips. In these types of waters many lures can be used with varying degrees of success but none has proven more effective over the last half century than a darter. More fish are landed at

Montauk Point during night time hours on darters than all other lures combined. I personally usually carry at least a dozen darters in various colors in my surf bag when fishing these areas. In the fall when fishing really heats up on these shores it is sometimes difficult not to use a darter at night. Faced with crowded conditions one must do what others are doing and if you try to use a lure with a different retrieve speed you will end up crossing everyone's line. Since most guys will be tossing darters you really have no choice but to follow their lead. Thankfully, Montauk Point is a large place and if you seek solitary conditions all you have to do is walk away from the crowds or better yet, fish late into the night. But I do have to question. Why in the world would you come to Montauk and not want to use a darter?

Darters also work great darting amongst rocks in the dark.

As recently as ten years ago, New York beaches and Montauk Point, in particular, were the epicenter of darter activity on the east coast. The darter was such a local lure that one manufacturer commented: "I can't give them away west, north or south of Montauk". Boy, how quickly the times have changed. Anglers have now realized that fast water in Montauk Point has the same property as fast waters in New Jersey, Maine or Rhode Island and that darters are just as effective as they are at the Point. Granted, very few anglers gave up all their gear and stuffed their bags with darters but many now have another weapon to use on their fish seeking expeditions. I must admit, I readily toss a darter on a sandy beach that borders an inlet or off an inlet jetty as I do a hundred miles away in Montauk Point. The beaches that border the western side of inlets benefit greatly by the ebbing current coming out of these inlets. These are the areas where baitfish will be flushed out of the back bays by outgoing currents or where bait fish will congregate for their fall migrations to southern waters. It is here where predators will lurk to find the bait fish as they leave the friendly and protected confines of the back bays and harbors. The outgoing current will act as a funnel to concentrate bait in these locations. Of course, our job is to find exactly where and when this happens. Open beaches which are too far from the inlet to benefit from the inlet current are generally poor places to cast a darter with one exception. During stormy conditions when there is a prolonged period of strong wind from one direction a "sweep" will be created along the beach. An angler can use this sweep in a similar manner as he uses the natural current flow.

COLOR ME BLIND...

When it comes to choosing which color darter to use, follow the lead of Montauk rock hoppers who would not dream of getting on their rock without a few yellow darters in their surf bag. Some claim that the fascination with yellow darters goes back to the days when hordes of juvenile weakfish were often found shining their golden colors in the Montauk surf. Others argue that because the Montauk bottom is covered with kelp all baitfish appear yellow-ish in its water. I don't know which of these theories might be right. However, there probably is a little truth in both. But, why then are yellow darters so effective on sandy beaches close to home where I fish? I learned a long time ago to let the fish decide what they want to hit instead of trying to force-feed them the color that I might think they want. In my experience the yellow darter is what fish prefer more often than any other pattern. Who am I to argue? You could follow the traditional "light on light nights, dark on the dark nights" approach. Frankly, I never found this concept to be anything but a crapshoot. I fish yellow and white plugs as much in the daytime as I do at night and they are my primary colors regardless of what lure I use. Besides, I've been burned too many times with the aforementioned approach that I won't even consider it when I pick my colors. I guess you could use it as a starting point in your exploration but I would not get married to the concept and I'll tell you why. A few years ago my good friend Scott Cunningham joined me for night fishing in Montauk. Since he just drove for three hours to get there and it was his birthday I wanted to put him onto some fish. It

Fishing during hours of darkness is a key when using a darter.

was a night with a new moon that I won't soon forget. It was so dark we could not see each other as we were suiting up next to my truck. We started at one of Montauk's most fabled locations, the rip at False Bar located on the north side of the lighthouse. The tide was receding and the ebbing current was picking up speed. We were joined in the water by about a dozen other surfcasters. I would not describe it as crowded, but just comfortable enough to be uncomfortable if any decent size fish decided to show up, if you know what I mean. Unfortunately, the stripers either did not read the new moon chapter in many fishing books or someone tipped them off about our intentions, either way they failed to show up. I managed a lone schoolie on a white darter and after about an hour I told my buddy I would walk north about a hundred yards and try North Bar. I got there and almost bumped into two fellows standing knee deep in the water. Not quite understanding why they didn't push further into the water, I waded past them till I was in the water up to my waist. Feeling good about the location I had chosen, I made a cast with the white darter that earlier had enticed the schoolie since it was still hanging from the end of my leader. Before I even made a single turn on the reel handle, a mountain of white water appeared out of the darkness and swept me off of my feet. Now I realized why the other two anglers were standing in the water up to their knees. Here I was tumbling in the surf and imagining the smile on the faces of the other two guys and praying that I did not crack my head on a rock or even worse, break my rod or my reel. After being pushed several yards backwards I regained my composure and gingerly attempted to get up. At I was shifting my feet and trying to move bowling ball size rocks from under my feet so I could achieve a stable fishing platform from which to launch my next cast. At the same time I was trying to regain my line before it got hopelessly tangled in and around the boulders. Doing my best to stay on my feet I finally picked up all the slack only to find that my plug was stuck. I leaned backwards and yanked on my rod only to find myself being pulled forward. The rock moved! Unable to get my feet set I flew head first into the water almost being dragged by what was now obviously a fish. Now I was pissed! I got up with determination to stop this embarrassment, only to find another wall of white water barreling towards me. Talk about "googanism" at its best! Holy crap, did I take a beating that night. Finally I landed the darn fish, re-checked my snap and made another cast. At this point the current was moving at full force and I was losing my conviction we were going to find some fish when my darter gets slammed in the rip and the fish takes off peeling drag with the current. In the next half an hour I landed another four quality stripers and all on a white darter. I tried blurple (black over purple), yellow and black but could not buy a bump. After about a half an hour of inaction I waded back to the beach. The anglers I had passed on the way out were still standing in the same spot. One of them yelled, as I passed by at a distance not able to see who it was, "We see you got fish. What did you get them on?"." A white darter", I yelled back and disappeared into the darkness. Since nothing really was happening at False Bar I suggested to Scott that we try Jones Reef which was a few hundred yards to the southeast of where we where, towards the lighthouse. At this point it was well after midnight and one lowly truck was parked at the reef. We waded into the water and I found some rocks to stand on. Since it was his birthday I gave him the flat one and I took the crappy one .It wasn't awful but I had to bend my knees together and then kind of flare my feet out. It was a very weird position, quite uncomfortable and very prone to getting washed off the rock. Let's just say I spent as much time that night getting on and off the rock as I did fishing. Thank the Lord that Scott's birthday doesn't come more than once a year! The white darter came through again with a dozen nice fish while my buddy had a few fish on a Sluggo rigged on a plain leadhead. After about an hour of fishing I was getting thirsty and decided to take a break. As I waded back to the shore a figure appeared out of the darkness and called me by name. Not sure who it was I waited for him to come face to face, finally

Using a straight retrieve is the most productive way to work a darter. In very fast moving water or during rough surf conditions give the lure a quick jerk with the rod after it has landed in the water. This helps a darter dig under the surface.

realizing it's my friend Paul. "Z" he said", "I only had one bass tonight and your light going on and off was driving me nuts. You must have landed a dozen fish. What the heck were you throwing?" My reply was "a white darter". I might as well have told him I was casting a golden fork with hooks on it because he probably would have been less surprised. He shook his head in disbelief and said," You kidding me? White on a new moon? I got every color darter in my bag except.....white". The next morning as I stopped in town to get my fill of coffee I ran into two fellow High Hill Striper Club members. They informed me that they fished the bars last night but they had not got as much as a bump. However, they reported that there was a madman that waded passed them that almost got killed by waves, but he was catching fish. Before they finished the rest of the story I asked them, "So, how many white darters you bought this morning?" Not able to hold it in I busted out laughing and revealed who the dark stranger was that walked past them in the night. As you can see, rules are made to be broken. What works tonight might not work tomorrow. When it comes to darters I will always take the yellow one out of the bag first. If that doesn't work I will go with either two extremes, black and/or white. To me it doesn't get any more basic than this. At this point; if I fail to entice a strike then, blurple, gold or even pink might make an appearance. By the way, pink darters with their zigzag motion are an excellent imitation of squid. This is especially true if you add to their natural action short bursts of speed with your reel or a sweep of your rod. This action mimics a squid's swimming style. Adding a long pink feather on the back treble enhances the simulation of squid tentacles.

RETRIEVE

The darter is almost exclusively a night lure and its effectiveness in the daytime is reduced to such an extent that it is not even worth trying. Trust me on this one. I went through a period of wanting to prove to everybody how wrong they were, but I failed. The fish have voted with their lack of interest so stick to popping plugs, metal lips and bucktails in day time. Retrieving a darter is pretty much a straight forward process. Cast it up tide and retrieve just fast enough to feel the resistance of the moving water. Obviously the actual strength of the current will influence the speed of your retrieve. Some surfcasters like to add a little embellishment to their retrieve but this is usually reserved for those nights when the action is slow. On bright full moon nights cast your darter up tide and before starting the retrieve, start shaking your rod tip as if you were working a pencil popper. The point of this exercise is to draw the fish into the vicinity of the lure and then have them attack it once a normal retrieve is initiated. Another trick to try, if you are using a spinning reel, is to extend the index finger of your hand to interrupt the retrieval of the line while you are reeling. The line will slap against your finger during the retrieve and it will impart an erratic action on the lure as it moves through the water. I reserve these types of retrieves for slow nights or when I am getting light bumps but not actually hooking up. Most of the time, after a cast I'll give a plug a little jerk to get under the surface and then just retrieve only as fast as the current "lets" me. Yes, the water will talk to you if you open your mind enough in to hear it and this just doesn't apply to darters but to all lures we use. Water movement and not wind, bait or structure will determine at which speed or manner we should retrieve our lures in order for them to be effective. In the case of a darter, once resistance is felt just reel fast enough to keep that tension with the lure. Once your darter has washed out of the rip you'll feel that resistance has been lost at which point reel like a madman before you tangle with the guy next to you. Hey, I didn't say it was easy, just fun. At times of slower water movement, I like to embellish my retrieve a little by either speeding it up to make the darter swim a bit faster or use a sweep of my rod to produce a similar effect. I never found that this works as well as a straight retrieve during fast water movement but it is effective at times.

SIZE THEM UP

There is a lure called the Yo-Zuri Mag Darter which in addition to being made out of plastic ingeniously has a sliding weight in its belly. The weight slides to its tail by the force generated during the cast. Even though this is a smaller version of a darter you can achieve some pretty impressive casting distances considering its size and the weight transfer system. Although I can wholeheartedly recommend these lures and they are probably my number one weapon when chasing August weakfish, they really can't be considered "darters". They are really swimming plugs with a slight darting action but take my word for it, they are deadly in the surf. In addition to using them in the summer, because they cast so well, I also toss them in the ocean surf early in the year when the diet of stripers and blues consists primarily of smaller baitfish. When it comes to picking the size for a darter, the surfcaster has even less of a choice than when picking a brand. Super Strike makes a single 2 3/8 ounce model while Gibbs darters range in size from 1 5/8 to 3 ounces. If I had to pick only one darter with which to fish with, Super Strike darter would get the nod. Brilliantly designed and virtually indestructible these darters swim true right out of the package. Tattoo and Beachmaster make a 3 ounce model sporadically while Beachmaster also has a fat and short 2 ounce model. Although Choopy and L.I.FISH IN VT are relative newcomers compared to established brands they have quickly gained a following among the surf crowd for their quality construction and of course, their fish catching ability. My belief is weight is not as important as the length of the darter. I find darters between 6 and 8 inches in length to be the most appealing to the fish.

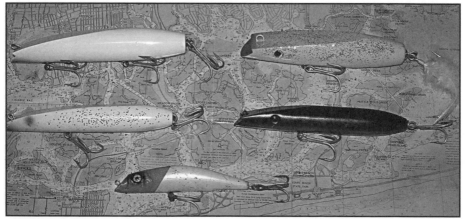

Some of today's most popular darters.

I can cast them with ease and their long profile attracts good size fish. Interestingly, I also find that the longer darters do not discourage the smaller fish. What more can you ask from a plug?

TIP

For a better "dig" or action in rough surf replace the front 3/0 treble hook with a 4/0 treble. Remove the treble from the back of the darter and replace it with a single bucktailed or feathered hook attached via a split ring. The split ring will allow the hook to fold against the body of the lure during the cast. In addition, you won't have to deal with trebles when those pesky bluefish chomp on the rear of your plug. This modification also works well on most other lures.

CHAPTER TEN

— NEEDLEFISH —

My introduction to needlefish lures happened innocently enough during a June new moon some years ago. At two hundred and forty pounds and 6 foot 3 inches tall, I have a hard time sneaking up on anyone, yet on this dark night the three guys already in the water did not even turn around as I joined them. The fact that each one of them had a bent rod might have had something to do with it. Excitedly I attached a yellow darter to my snap and made a cast into the darkness. As the fast moving water washed over the face of the darter, the lure started to move in a zigzag pattern and I readied myself for an immediate pick up by a hungry bass. I knew they were still there since the three guys were again hooked up in unison. Surprisingly, I got no bumps so I made another cast but I drew the same result. One cast after another found a similar fate. It quickly became apparent that I was casting the "wrong lure", as my hookup ratio to theirs was about one in ten. As the night was so dark I could hardly make out the shape of the guys, never mind what they were casting. I thought about similar circumstances I had found myself in a few nights before. I was fishing a jetty rip from the shore and a boat was anchored on the outside of the rip, maybe 30 yards away. I was hooking into weakfish on just about every cast, while the fellow in the boat was drawing blanks. Finally he purposely made a cast over my line and tangled me up so he could see what I was tossing. Knowing how upset I was at that guy, I rejected the notion of doing the same thing to the guys next to me. So I walked out of the water, unnoticed by them, just as I had arrived and left the scene.

The next day a friend informed me he was one of the three guys I had seen the night before doing a number on bass. "What the heck were you throwing?" I said, thinking they had some super secret lure in their possession. "Needlefish" he answered. The bells started to ring in my head. Of course, the water must have been loaded with sand eels. I thanked him for his honesty and walked, no, I ran to my truck to restock my lure bag and then shot back to the scene of the crime, impatiently waiting for the tide to turn. I was the first one there and I entered the water eagerly only to be startled by the sight of fish busting in front of my boots. I don't know who was startled more, the fish or me but I froze for a moment until my heart rate dropped to an acceptable level. I quietly and slowly as my klutzy body would allow me, retraced my steps back onto dry land and made a short cast of about 15 yards. One turn of the handle was all it took before the bass swallowed the needlefish and started thrashing his tail in the shallow waters. I caught a glimpse of my buddy about to enter the water when I called him over." Whatever you do, do not get into the water. They are feeding 15 yards away, just cast from the shore". Boy, did we have a ball that night. Bass after bass were committing suicide on anything that resembled a needlefish. They were chasing sand eels almost onto the rocky beach. Nights like this can go a long way to instilling confidence in such an oddly shaped lure such as needlefish.

A LITTLE HISTORY...

From a historical perspective the needlefish lure is a relative newcomer on the surf fishing scene. Its early beginning's can be traced to the Boone Co. They made screwed eye models designed for casting and attracting warm water species in the southwestern part of the country. According to those who remember, there were very few anglers that used these or any other needlefish style lures before the 1980's. Then a series of events happened and ushered in what many believe to be, the greatest decade of large striper fishing in history. Large schools of truly big stripers could be found gorging on hordes of large sand eels in the surf from the rocky shorelines of Montauk Point to the sandy beaches of Cape Cod. Forty pound bass barely elicited a raised eyebrow. This was not surprising considering the fact that bass over fifty pounds, the magic mark, were brought to the market daily. Block Island in particular became the epicen-

Needlefish are one of the most productive night lures regardless of location.

ter of this activity but unless you were in the "circle of trust" you had a very slim chance of finding out about it. Tight lips were the norm on Block Island because of sheer competitiveness and the fact that most of these fish ended up sold. Few guys wanted to risk the wrath of their fellow surfcasters by blowing the lid off the pot. Stories abound about surfcasters tripping over "logs" in the darkness only to find out when they turned on their lights that the high water mark was littered with cow stripers. Since sand eels (which by all accounts were very large) were thought to be the bait fish responsible for drawing these great hordes of large stripers within casting range of the shore bound anglers, it was only natural that the surfcasters themselves were looking for a lure that would closely imitate this forage fish. Some say it was Boone's while others say it was needles made by a company by the name of Classic from New Jersey that first appeared in the surf. Regardless of which was first, neither one proved to withstand the punishment these large stripers were able to dish out. Boone had screw-on eyes and according to many accounts after each fish anglers would have to re-tighten the screws to the body. In addition, these plugs were fairly light and they were hard to cast in any onshore wind. About the same time, Don Musso, designer of the Super Strike line of wood lures heard about this great mass of sand eels along the coast and how effective these fragile needlefish were. He however had no knowledge of what these lures looked like other than what was described to him over the phone. Then one day while browsing through a saltwater magazine he stumbled onto an advertisement for the Boone needlefish. His designer juices were already stroked by all the action that was taking place on Block Island, but now he had a mental picture of the lure. Don came up with his own version, tapered on both ends unlike anything anyone had ever seen before. In addition, for the first time in history, the needlefish lure was made through-wired. A problem surfaced almost immediately as big bass were pulling 60lb swivels out with ease. He upped it to a 90 lb swivel but that still wasn't enough and he finally settled on a 150 lb swivel. The lures were so popular that very few of them ever actually made it onto the store shelves; most were grabbed out of the box as soon as Don would put them on the tackle store counter. A year or so later Super Strike stopped making wooden lures and switched production to plastic. Even though the switch from wood to plastic cut the time it took to make each lure, for a long period afterwards Don could not keep up with the demand. Not surprisingly when you consider that every issue of The Fisherman magazine in those days had reports of big fish being landed and more times than not they were caught on needlefish lures. This great run petered out after a few years but needlefish lures continued to produce even though sand eels were never as abundant or large after those banner years. The ensuing years brought a collapse in the striped bass population and a moratorium on the fishery. The needlefish lure had some of the wind taken out of its sails.

At this point, many anglers who had supplemented their income selling fish just stopped fishing altogether. The occasional fisherman soaked bait as bass were hard to find using plugs. Fortunately the striped bass stocks have recovered and in the late 90's some notable catches on Hab's needlefish generated renewed interest in this lure. John Habrek, the designer of Hab's lures, became a household name in surf

Some of today's most popular needlefish lures.

fishing circles. Looking at the profile of a needlefish one might question why a "stick with hooks" as some have called it would elicit so much interest from gamefish. After all, sand eels are seasonal baitfish in most places and in some years their presence is barely noticeable. Yet needlefish lures continue to produce good catches throughout the whole season. The actual art of casting and catching fish might be simple. But it is hard to figure out exactly why this lure is productive when the baitfish that it is suppose to imitate is not present.

Needlefish lures might have gotten their humble start by the desire of surfcasters to imitate sand eels. But, there are other baitfish in our waters that have long, slim bodies such as large spearing, eels, garfish, and real needlefish. These are just a few of the items any striper would love to have on its menu. Additionally, who would argue that adding a plastic skirt or long feathers to a needlefish lure does not make a great imitation of a pulsating, defensive squid ? Not I. As you can tell, there is more that meets the eye floating under the surface in this great ocean of ours. In addition these lures can be fished in just about any conditions as they will cut through the strongest wind with ease and can be worked at different depths by simply adjusting the speed of the retrieve. You get a sense that a "stick with hooks" is a lot more versatile than it appears at first glance. In fact the only limit on how to work your needlefish might be your own imagination. Dragging a needlefish lure through the sand with intermittent puffs makes for a deadly sand eel imitation. Work it in mid-depth in anticipation that a gamefish will mistake it for an eel or a real needlefish. Some anglers have even resorted to working it over the top like a pencil popper in the spring. Early in the year the fish often key in on smaller baits and will strike at needlefish worked this way while ignoring large pencil poppers that produce so well in the fall months.

I like to work my needlefish with a slight flick of the wrist every few cranks of the reel while some of my friends like to employ long sweeps of the rods after which they quickly pick up the slack. The fish will often strike the lure the same way after either motion, as it flutters towards the bottom like an injured and dying baitfish. Now I've caught fish by utilizing all of these techniques, twitching, sweeping, dragging it on the bottom or working it over the top but there is no technique that has proven more successful over the years than a slow and straight retrieve. "What?", You ask,

Not one but two bluefish fell for this needlefish worked over the top like a pencil popper early in the season.

"You expect me to believe that a lure with no built in action of its own, no metal lip, no slope like a darter or the concave face of a popper is most productive when retrieved slow AND straight ?" You are forgetting two very important things when it comes to presentation of this lure: current sweep and wave action. Either one will have a tremendous effect on how the lure appears under water and must be taken into consideration when working any lure. So yes, the slow and straight retrieve is probably the most productive retrieve when using these lures. I think it's fair to say that no lure will catch fish at all times but darned if the needlefish doesn't come close. The only exception that I can think of is during times of slack or non-moving water. Then again, there are not many lures that exactly excel under these conditions. Over the years I found most success with these lures either in fast moving waters or when there is a nice roll of white water present on ocean front beaches.

As with most lures we use, it's important to cast it up tide in order to present our offering in a most lifelike manner. Remember, baitfish are influenced by current too and our mission is to present our lure in such a manner that the gamefish will mistake it for the real thing. When fishing in fast moving water around the inlets or places like Montauk Point, where great amounts of water are displaced every change of the tide, I find the straight and steady retrieve elicits the most strikes. When fishing white water conditions on oceanfront beaches, I find that a bit of finesse is usually required on the part of the angler. I like to keep my needlefish on the backside of a wave as long as possible as I find that most of the hits occur when the lure is worked through the foamy residue on the wave's backside. Stripers and blues in particular are fond of feeding in the turbulence waves create and I like to keep my lure in the most turbulent part of the wave as long as possible. The reason this "washing machine" like turbulence is so appealing to the gamefish is that although they cruise through it with ease, baitfish and small sea creatures are at the mercy of the turbulence.

Needlefish lures are primarily a night lure as they are not nearly as productive in daytime as they are under the cover of darkness. This of course makes the art of the retrieve strictly based on feel as opposed to visual contact. The retrieve, as with most plugs used in the dark, should be kept as slow as possible without hitting the bottom unless you intend to stir up some sand, in which case, knock yourself out. Sometimes an agonizingly slow speed, especially on a night when fishing is poor, will test your mettle and you will be second guessing your choice of lures. It happens to me occasionally but each time it does I remember the advice I received from John Habrek a few years ago. I asked him to sum up for me his idea of how needlefish lures should be fished. He replied: "Z, if you are not bored fishing a needlefish, you are doing it wrong". Sadly, John Habrek passed away only few days after finishing reading the manuscript of this book. He called me excitedly to give me his review of the book and was ecstatic that a book about lures was in the making. One of the most entertaining plug builders in the industry, John was wildly respected for his workmanship and was a great ambassador for the sport of surfcasting. Hab's lures will remain a benchmark of quality and design for many years to come.

Until a few years ago anglers had few choices when it came to choosing which needlefish to buy. Super Strike and Gibbs were widely available while Habs and Beachmaster were harder to find than weapons of mass destruction. These days more and more builders are jumping into the fray and today's angler has many lures to choose from in this category. Al Gags has resurrected his line of fine lures; J.N-SKI and Fixter make quality custom needles that can be designed to your specifications. One of my favorites of these newer products is made by Don Guimelli of Afterhours lures. I find his color schemes very much to my liking and his squid pat-

Needlefish lures make great eel skin plugs.

tern needle is a dead ringer for the real thing. Some builders like Choopy lures even make a floating version which leaves a very nice wake on the surface. Having said that I still reach for my trusted Super Strike yellow needlefish eight out of ten times. If I had to pick my favorite size needle I would go with one that weighs in between 1.5 and 2.5 ounces and is about 7 inches in length, with moderate sink rate. Needlefish lures in this size and weight range cast like a bullet and can be used year around with efficacy.

In addition, I find this size to be very appealing to the fish from late spring all the way into November. Smaller versions I generally find too light to use in the ocean. They are more productive in the protected waters of the back bays or Long Island Sound. The truly large version like the old Super Strike Wads or Hab's 9 inch models are great if you are looking to cull some bigger fish out of the school as they present a large target to those big girls that generally don't like to feed on tiny meals. It is hard to generalize where each lure is most effective and in which size as no two needlefish lures are alike even though they might be the same size. Think of my advice as a starting point in your needlefish adventure. I'll let you write the final chapter.

TIP

Load a Super Strike needlefish with either water or small lead pellets by drilling a hole in the rear chamber or by using a hot nail to penetrate the plastic. Modified in this manner it becomes a great plug to use in big seas and strong head-on winds. In addition, if you are planning to fish in very deep rips you can load it up to 3 or 4 ounces and get it down deep in the water column. Because their weight is in the rear these loaded needles become very good casting plugs and the weight helps keep the nose of the plug up in rocky areas. Seal the plug by either applying silicone or just melting the plastic around the hole with a hot nail until you close it up.

CHAPTER ELEVEN

— POPPING PLUGS —

E nticing a striper or a bluefish to rise from the depths and take a swipe at a popper could be called the ultimate accomplishment for any surfcaster. After all, these feisty gamefish find the bottom contour much more appealing than cruising on the surface. Observing them slash, swirl and at times clear water completely in pursuit of a surface lure has left me many times in awe of their aggressiveness. Popping plugs are usually the lure that gets fish so agitated that they are known to occasionally chase the plug right onto the beach, not realizing they are running out of water. These types of lures might be great at raising the fish's blood pressure but are not nearly as effective in actually hooking them. This is partly because of the plug's side to side movement and partly because of the higher speed of retrieve used by many anglers when fishing with these plugs. The fish chasing the plug often lunges at the plug but finds that the lure that was there a moment ago is now a few feet away.

There are various types of popping plugs but two in my opinion are superior to any others on the market today. They are the standard popper and the pencil popper. Although they are all surface lures they are vastly different due to the retrieves used and the movements they make. Standard poppers and pencil poppers are by far the most popular styles but their only common bond is the ability of a surfcaster to cast them great distances.

POPPERS

Standard poppers come in many shapes and sizes but one characteristic they all have in common is a scooped out front of the plug. This particular feature is what makes a popper "pop" as water is displaced out of the concave cavity as the surfcaster jerks his rod tip backwards. The splashing that these lures make is very effective in arousing the curiosity of gamefish which will often approach the lure after they sense the initial splash. This activity imparted to the lure by the angler causes the popper to imitate a wounded bait fish struggling on the surface, sending this message to the predator, "I am an easy meal." Many times fish are attracted by the splashing and are ready to strike but still not committed yet. So they trail the lure and the moment a surfcaster pops the lure again the fish's instinct takes over and they attack it. This is the primary reason why popping plugs should not be skipped across the surface at lightning speed but instead retrieved as slowly as possible with intermittent pops, giving the game fish a chance to catch up with the plug and strike it. The angler should generate a rhythmic cadence such as pop, pop, pause or pop, pop, pop, pause. The reason for this is that cold water species are not usually known to chase a surface lure at high speed like their warmer water cousins. Therefore, the pause in the popping gives the predator a chance to catch the plug.

When choosing a standard popper you will be faced with the decision to either use a floating or a sinking model. For example, Gibbs' old-time favorite Polaris popper is a floating popper made of wood that will rest on the surface after a cast. Super Strike makes both a sinking version of their Little Neck Popper and a floating version. You can identify the sinking model by the black eyes and the floating model by the green eyes. The sinking version will head for the bottom as soon as it hits the water. These two plugs were designed to produce similar actions on the surface yet they are vastly different in the way they can be retrieved.

The floating poppers are a bit more versatile in my opinion than the sinking models, but I think the sinking ones are more effective. I generally do not carry many floaters in my bag unless I know that there is a lot of weed in the water, the surf is flat or the fish have been fussy. Certain places get weeded out on a regular basis while others only around the periods of a full or new moon. When weed is thick in the surf, the floating popper is often the only lure that can be used effectively. Most sinking lures will pick up weed on the trebles immediately upon entering the water rendering them useless. Floating poppers stay on the surface during the retrieve, suspended above the weed. When the surf is calm, fish often become fussy feeders and though they might rise to the surface and follow the lure, very often they will turn away without taking a swipe. In these situations I find floating poppers very effective, as I can work them with a "stop and go" retrieve. Unlike the sinking models that will head for the bottom if you stop your retrieve, the floaters can be manipulated in order to entice a strike from a fish that is not really in the a feeding mode.

Regular popping retrieves which are fine when the fish are aggressive rarely work when fish are fussy. I find sloshing the floater through the surface and then letting it rest for a few seconds is much more productive than a reel, pop, reel, the most commonly used retrieve. The gamefish, although hidden from our view, are

Work your poppers slowly and deliberately, especially if you are targeting striped bass.

attracted to the splashing of the lure but if they are not in a feeding mood, they might just follow it out of curiosity. If the lure is continuously moving away they will eventually turn away and head back to deeper water. With a stop and go retrieve, the fish will instinctively and at times, reflexively lunge at the lure even though they show no signs of aggressive feeding. Seeing a meal, that just appeared dead and motionless on the surface, begin to move is usually too tempting for stripers to resist. I said stripers because bluefish usually do not show as much patience when it comes to their feeding habits. They will either move in for the kill immediately or they will swim past the lure. Their tendency is to chase down the baitfish instead of ambushing it like stripers. This behavior on the part of bluefish

143

supports the notion that they prefer a slightly faster retrieve than stripers. This is true but in a twisted way like everything else in this sport. Bluefish in my opinion prefer a continuously moving target but not necessarily at high speed.

The sinking poppers are, in my humble opinion, a bit misunderstood especially by those who have recently joined the ranks of surfcasters. One might think that because they sink an angler might have a hard time keeping them on the surface, but this is not true. Retrieving with a moderate speed while employing a jerk of the rod every few turns of the reel, keeps these poppers chugging along. The reason I mentioned previously that they are more productive than floating poppers is precisely because they sink. Once you pop the lure it will flutter backwards under the surface just like a dying baitfish does after it has lost its strength. Have you ever seen an injured or dying fish in an aquarium or a fish tank as it struggles towards the surface? Eventually it gives up and allows its body to start fluttering towards the bottom. The sinking poppers almost imitate this motion to a tee and stripers will often attack the lure on either the fall from the surface or immediately after it shows renewed signs of life. In a fish's mind this signals that the prey has detected them and is trying to get away. Rarely will you see them chasing a lure rapidly skipping over the surface. Again, when we present our lure we always must take into the account the way gamefish feed and the style of ambush they prefer. If you are intendingto strictly go after blues, by all means speed up your retrieve slightly but be forewarned that you will often eliminate any chance of a striper going after your lure.

I like bright colors on my poppers, primarily yellow, hot pink, parrot or just plain white. I feel that these colors are most effective in attracting fish on ocean beaches where water visibility is usually reduced by moving

Super Strike Little Neck, today's most popular popper.

sand. I want my lure to stand out as much as possible. Add to the equation the white, foamy water that often rolls over the bar and the visibility of your lure will be reduced even further. This is not to say that, with this particular style of lure, colors have an overwhelming influence on one's success. Not at all! I think the commotion these lures create will draw the fish to the lure and the proper retrieve, depending on conditions, will be the reason they decide to strike it or not. Still, I've done better with these colors than with any others over the years. Super Strike sinking 2 3/8 Little Neck poppers are by far my favorites in this category. Other leading manufacturers include Gibbs, Atom, Saltybugger, Yo-Zuri, Storm and Tsunami.

PENCIL POPPERS

As he got older, legendary Massachusetts plug builder Stan Gibbs was frustrated that he could not reach the fish younger and stronger surfcasters were reaching so he designed a plug that would outcast all plugs. According to legend, his frustration gave birth to the first pencil popper that has evolved into the lure known today as the Gibbs Canal Special. It is flat on the bottom and has a heavy weight in the tail. This design makes them plane better in the fast waters of the Cape Cod Canal and they also cut through the air with ease. Thus they are capable of reaching the fish that were previously out of casting range.

Today's surfcaster has so many models and manufacturers to choose from that it might inspire a "paralysis by analysis" in trying to pick one to use. Fortunately, most are similar in shape and Stan's original design has proven to withstand the test of time remarkably well. Most pencil poppers on the market today are round in shape, with a bowling pin like bottom and featuring elongated necks. Most of the weight is concentrated in the tail and that is what makes these plugs cast like a rocket. The long neck serves as a primary attractant to the fish as it slaps water side to side, while the bottom stays more or less stationary in a pivoting motion just under the surface. The time honored way to properly work a pencil popper is to place your rod butt between your knees and with your right hand grab the rod a few inches under the first guide. Then violently start to whip or shake the rod tip back and forth, away and then towards your body, while at the same time reeling just fast enough to keep in contact with the plug. Fortunately (or unfortunately, depending to which camp you belong) fiberglass rods that were so good at whipping up a frenzy with pencil poppers have been replaced by stiffer graphite models. However, with the new braided lines, graphite rods can produce a similar action as described previously by just sliding the right hand slightly above the reel or even just holding it at the reel stem. The furious wiping motion of parabolic fiberglass rods is now replaced by the tighter but more intense back and forth action of graphite rods. When the rod is worked in this manner the pencil popper slaps the water side-to-side as is it moving slowly forward. One should never reel in more than just the slack in the line and one should never, ever try to set the hook on the attacking fish. Why? Since the rod is whipping back and forth in order to make the plug work, if you try to "set" the hook the only thing you will accomplish is pulling the plug away from the fish. The end result is that the fish will probably lose interest and swim away. I know you need nerves of steel not to try setting the hook on a fish that is exploding on your lure, but trust me; your rod will do it for you. As the fish gets a hold of the plug the natural whipping action of the rod will set the hook every time. All you have to do is tighten the line and if you are like me, set the hook one more time, making sure the hooks penetrate its jaw. Since

This large bass fell to a pencil popper on a sandy beach.

these plugs whip side to side very violently, if your retrieve is too fast bass or even bluefish will have a hard time getting their jaws around it. Cranking the reel just fast enough to pick up slack and keep in contact with the plug is often the ticket to success. These lures are excellent "fish finders." By that I mean they are very good at attracting fish to the commotion and telling us if there are fish in the area. Pencil poppers are often the first lure I will use when I am starting to work a particular piece of structure. Quite often I will raise fish but not manage to hook up. If I don't get a strike on the next series of casts, I might throw a metal lip swimmer or a standard popper in the area hoping to entice the fish to strike something a little different. In addition, they are very good at enticing very large stripers to the surface as their side to side action moves lots of water. As a result this action prevents the big cows from having a clear view of exactly what they are attacking. Smaller sizes, up to 2 ounces are more productive in the spring or summer, while large 3 to 4 ounce models rule in the fall when gamefish are zoning in on the larger size baits that are prevalent.

My favorite pencil poppers are Surface Cruisers by Yo-Zuri, even though I have to replace the split rings that come with them and the fact that the paint chips way too easily. However, I have found that they are easy to work and no pencil popper I have ever used dances quite like it. Just like standard poppers, I like to work them on the ocean front beaches when there is a good deal of white water present. I will often adjust my retrieve or stop retrieving completely if necessary just so I can work my plug over the incoming wave and slide it on the backside. Once I know the plug is in the foam behind the wave, I will accelerate the whipping motion even though I usually can't see the plug behind the wave. It is when the plug is in this area that I will often get hits. I apologize if I sound like a broken record but white water and aggressive feeding fish go together like peanut butter and jelly. You could eat one without the other, but why? The same is true for foamy surf. You can catch fish in calmer ocean waters but you will never find the fish as aggressive as you do when there is a good roll coming over the sandbar. The exception to this rule is deep water inlets or breachways where current affects the manner in which the gamefish might feed. Gibbs pencil poppers have probably caught more fish than all other pencil poppers combined so take that into account when planning your next purchase. Other well regarded builders include Plugcaster which is quickly becoming one of my favorites, Gag's, Saltybugger, Habs, Afterhours, Eel Punt and Big Don. In summer months snappers or juvenile bluefish raise a ruckus and often break water in the process, in the back bays, chasing spearing. This in turn draws in stripers who are attracted by the mayhem schools of snappers create. Since the stripers are already zoning in on the surface a pencil popper becomes a very effective way to get them fooled into thinking it's a real meal.

Cotton Cordell's pencil poppers feature a rattle inside their plastic body and are very effective in drawing stripers to the surface, especially in calmer waters. On ocean front beaches the rattle looses its effectiveness but the plugs still produce. My favorite places for working a pencil popper are boulder strewn areas where there is always lots of resident bait present. Blackfish, scup, bergals and other small crustaceans all seek shelter among the rocks and this in turn draws resident stripers in the area. I like to work my pencil popper over each boulder by casting at different angles

before I move on to the next rock. Usually you can find a fish or two holding behind the structure waiting to ambush. As the pencil popper reaches their strike zone they will make a strong push with their tails and zoom to the surface but unlike the stripers that are cruising the open beach these stripers will usually not give you a second chance if they miss the first time. They just retreat back behind a boulder; waiting for the next opportunity to ambush its prey.

I find that regardless of where I fish pencil poppers and I have fished them from New Jersey to Massachusetts, dawn is the by far the most productive

Another quality bass that was fooled by a dancing pencil popper.

time to use them. Dusk is a bit overrated in my opinion as boat traffic, surfers, swimmers and sun worshipers all play their part in keeping the fish away at this time. If you are new to the sport or your free time is strictly limited to the daytime hours, this is one lure you must have in your surf bag.

Standard poppers and pencil poppers are primarily daytime lures and they lose most of their effectiveness in the dark. However, there are a few situations in which I have used them with success. For example, Super Strike Little Neck sinking, 2 3/8 ounce, poppers can be retrieved just under the surface and sometimes, when you need a long cast to reach the fish, this is the lure to do it with as it will outcast just about any lure in a similar size.

I find pencil poppers ineffective at night except for an occasional full moon period when it is so bright, night seems to turn into day. Even then the splashing these lures make can occasionally do more damage than good by spooking the fish especially if used in shallow water. I find surface swimmers to be more effective at night as they throw less water around in their wake. If you are an innovative type of a surfcaster who likes to go against the grain, feel free to experiment with poppers at night. I think you'll will find that although success is possible it is far from a sure thing. Considering how many proven night lures an angler has at his disposal these days and how limited we are by family and work obligations, popping at night is something I don't often do. But as soon as a little light begins to show in the east, I am ready! When dawn starts to show its colors and a new day is about to begin, you will find me on the beach sloshing my poppers over the sandbar in hope of hooking that cow of my dreams.

TIP

Try adding a large split ring on the nose wire of your pencil popper. The added room a split ring provides often results in exaggerated movement in the water, making your pencil popper a better "dancer". On poppers, replace the back treble with a single bucktail hook via a split ring. The split ring allows room for the hook to fold against the body during the cast, increasing your casting distance.

CHAPTER TWELVE

— METAL LIP SWIMME...

Early morning finds me standing in the water, fixated by the rising sun that is intent on painting the eastern sky red. The first flock of seagulls has risen from the sand and are nervously circling the surf line. My metal lip swimmer lands on the backside of a foamy wave and it starts to quiver in the receding water when I catch a glimpse of a large dorsal fin rising behind it. Then the broad shoulders of an angry striper appear, rising from beneath the surface and with its cavernous mouth wide open it propels itself through the white foam with a single swipe of its broad tail. The mayhem begins as the large striper has now realized why he never was a fan of wood or

The slow wobbling motion that metal lip swimmers produce account for many large stripers each year.

the hooks attached to it. The broom-like tail is furiously thrashing the surface in anger while he is trying to angle his body for a quick descent to the bottom. This scene has played out in my head so many times that I have a hard time separating fact from fiction. Sometimes I win, sometimes I lose. Then sometimes I just wake up too early to find out.

I am a little tired of hearing so called "experts" call metal lip swimmers "niche" lures. Not only are they not a niche lure, but in my view they are gle most important lure in a surfcaster's arsenal. How can I back up h a seemingly pretentious statement? The metal lip swimmer is the only lure that can be adjusted on the fly with a simple bend of the nose wire loop. They can be worked on the surface, subsurface and even in a deep water rip. But those are not the only reasons why I hold these lures in such high regard. An angler, who understands how and why metal lips work, is an angler who also understands the feeding habits of fish and how they relate to structure when on the feed. For me at least, no other lure has opened the window to the world of fish behavior more than metal lip swimmers.

Let the water" talk" to you when deciding whether to use either a surface or subsurface metal lip swimmer.

If I regard these lures so highly, why don't the "experts" share my opinion? First of all I don't consider myself an expert on anything and although I respect the time and effort others have logged on the beach, the truth is they are misinformed and quite frankly disinterested in this lure. I listened to a lecturer recently who told the audience that metal lips are all right when fish are aggressive and feeding on the top. You would think that this person, who has logged more years on the beach than I have been alive, would know all about metal lips. There are those that cast as well as darters and others that can reach the depth's where only bucktails usually venture. Is it ignorance? I don't know, but I can assure you, speaking from personal experience, the world of metal lip swimmers is vastly different than what it appears to be at first glance.

Granted, the majority of surfcasters today use these lures on the surface but this is not because they are murdering the fish on them, it's because they don't know any other way. In fact many would look at you with puzzlement if you told them you could bury a metal lip 15 feet under the surface. Years ago every jetty with a strong rip had a cadre of regulars whose primary weapons were Danny Pichney's Conrads and Slopeheads, both deep diving metal lips. With conventional rods and with reels filled with Dacron, they would cast their lures into the inlets and then allow another hundred yards to peel off the reel before engaging the reel and beginning a painfully slow retrieve while their plugs worked towards the bottom. Hundreds of cows fell for these plugs along the striper coast and many anglers made a name for themselves by primarily using deep diving metal lips.

In addition to the deep diving metal lip, there are the surface swimming varieties. None have proved more popular than Danny Pichney's namesake, the Danny plug. Brilliantly designed, this incredibly effective lure can be used under a variety of conditions and has a well earned reputation for catching big fish. Recently a new type of metal lip swimmer has hit the market from Beachmaster Lures simply named "Junior". From my point of view this is a very impressive plug. Designed with distance in mind, this particular lure is tail weighted and will outcast any metal lip on the market. It is a subsurface swimmer that is absolutely deadly on ocean beaches, and it is even more productive around inlets rips and jetties.

The most important part of choosing which metal lip to employ at any given time is letting the water "talk" to you. No, I have not lost my mind. I am referring to watching how the waves form or studying the current in a rip to determine the most likely place where the fish will be feeding. After all, casting a lure where the fish are not present is really a waste of time and time is something I don't like to waste. Choosing to go on top with a surface swimmer or under with a subsurface one is, in my opinion, the key to success when employing metal lips swimmers. I hope that I have aroused your curiosity about these lures. So now please allow me to try to explain why I think these lures are so versatile that you cannot afford to be without them.

SURFACE METAL LIP SWIMMERS

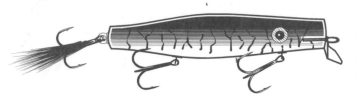

The knock on all metal lip swimmers is that they don't cast well. That is not a misconception but a fact. However you may not need to cast a metal lip very far at all. In addition, many surfcasters shy away from using metal lips when the wind is blowing in their face. By now you know how much I love to cast plugs in the white water but did you think about what conditions you need in order for white water to be created on the beaches? How about in your face wind? Would that help? The fact is, onshore winds push water over the sandbars and create white water. I love nothing more than a good moderate to stiff wind when fishing ocean beaches and I never found a wind to be a deterrent to my success when using metal lip swimmers. Furthermore, if the wind is onshore it will blow the bait tighter to the beach bringing the game fish closer, making long casts unnecessary. Besides, metal lips can only be cast so far regardless of your casting skills. Try to power cast a metal lip and it will probably tumble over itself so much that it will land at a shorter distance than if you used a moderate power cast. To use baseball terminology, take something off the fastball when you make a cast, somewhere between the lob cast for an eel and a power cast for a pencil popper. Then retrieve just enough until you feel the plug pulsating against the flow of the water.

My favorite surface metal lip swimmers are the ones that follow the design of the late Danny Pichney. Commonly known as a "Danny" plug, this lure is the most stable of any other surface lure that I have tried because it will not roll in the white water, where I like to cast them. I will use them under moderate to rough surf conditions including during Nor'easters in the fall. How do I manage to cast such a poor casting lure into a 40 MPH northeast wind? I don't. Instead I position myself on the western side of an inlet during an outgoing tide. The closer you get to an inlet the more likely you will encounter rough water that is more manageable. Standing on the west side of the inlet means that the wind will be coming over your left shoulder. All you have to do is angle your cast a little bit to the east and the wind will take the plug and carry it for you. It's a great way to cash in on the tendency of big fish to congregate around the inlets during a nor'easter especially if big bait is present at the time.

Although my favorite year round Danny style lure is a 6 inch model, in the spring and late fall, 7 or even 8 inch models are usually what it takes to get the attention of those large fish. I anticipate and enjoy so much fishing the nor'easters with metal lips that I even forgo the use of bucktails or needlefish in order to take advantage of the conditions these strong winds create. For most of the year however, I am happy to search for good white water on the beachfront in order to toss my surface metal lips. I find that it does not pay to cast these lures when the wind is at my back and the water is calm. On Long Island that means a wind from the north or

Although Danny type lures excel in the foamy white water along oceanfront beaches they are also deadly when retrieved slowly around boulders at night.

northwest. Interestingly enough it is during these conditions that a lot of surfcasters decide to use the metal lip in their bag because the wind will help carry the plug during the cast and provide for greater casting distance. Their idea is that the further they can cast, the more likely they will encounter a fish and have a hook up. On calmer days, I find that these types of plugs are marginally productive at best. I have had success at dawn under flat water conditions but I have had to adjust my retrieve in order to elicit some interest from the fish. Predatory fish are usually not as aggressive under these conditions. I find that "sloshing" my top water metal lip with a sweep of the rod will often entice a strike or at least draw some interest where a standard retrieve will usually result in getting skunked. As soon as my plug lands in the water I'll give it a "slosh" through the water causing it to dive under the water and then slowly rise to the surface. I then let it rest for a few seconds before starting my retrieve. Five or ten cranks later I might repeat this motion and then let the plug rest again for a moment.

You might pick off a few fish in the dark but I find fish are generally not feeding aggressively when there is no white water. Under calm conditions crabs, worms, clams and other crustaceans are all buried in the sand, the baitfish are spread along the beach and bass have to cruise the area in order to find food. In addition, calm conditions also give gamefish an opportunity to get really close to our lure, give it a long look and unfortunately, turn away most of the time. When white water is present all that changes. The crustaceans are exposed, the baitfish are tossed around and this veritable buffet stimulates bass and blues to move into the surf zone and feed. Now your plug that just landed in the white water foam is not that easily identified and often fish will hit on any motion in that part of the wave. If I am fishing a metal lip swimmer and white water is present I will zone in on the wave that is easily reachable with my cast. Considering that I am casting a metal lip, you know the cast will not be more than thirty or forty yards in distance. I will cast the lure as the wave is building; timing my cast so that it lands behind the breaking wave in the white water foam that it creates. If I don't get a hit by the time the foam starts to dissipate, which is probably not longer than twenty or 30 seconds, I reel quickly to retrieve line in order to be ready to do it again with the next wave. The period when the foam has dissipated, while I am in the process of retrieving the lure, is in my opinion the least productive part of the retrieve. I find that stripers like to rush into the foam, feed for a few moments and then retreat as the wave is receding. Keep in mind, this highly synchronized action takes place very quickly. Utilizing this technique depends on the proper wave formation, the height of the wave and the intervals between each wave. Hydrologists call this wave frequency. Sometimes I will try working consecutive waves where other times the waves do not come frequently enough to justify this method. I should mention that all waves and consequently all white water are not created equal. Sometimes you'll get that lazy roll over the sandbar where the wave kind of slowly folds onto itself. This is not the wave type that you want to fish. Forceful, wind driven waves that you know are carrying everything that happens to find itself in its path, is what I crave.

Although these plugs catch fish in the daytime they are even more productive during the night. At night an angler must rely on the rod to telegraph what his lure is doing and the seasoned angler will know when his plug is in the white water and when it is not. I suggest you get yourself familiar with these lures in the daytime. This is especially true if you need to make adjustments to improve the swimming action or the depth at which the plug swims. Remember under these conditions, when using this tactic it is important for the plug to be riding on the surface in the white water foam. Testing in daylight assures you of the correct action and placement, so at night you can fish with more confidence that you are doing everything right.

SO MANY PLUGS...SO LITTLE TIME

There are so many top water metal lip swimmers being made today that many surfcasters suffer from the "paralysis by analysis" syndrome. Having so many choices is a great thing if the products you have to choose from are worth your consideration. Personally, I have no desire to be the judge of what is good and what is not, neither do I claim to have tested every lure on the market but I do have some ideas as to what I am looking for in my metal lip swimmers.

First, I do not want a flimsy material for the metal lip as it will bend the first time I smack it into a rock, thus destroying the plugs action. Since I fish jetties a lot and my lures are in constant contact with boulders, mostly due to my incompetence, I want to make sure that the lip will not change its shape after contact. If yours does, then you may have just found the answer as to why on certain nights you could not buy a fish while others where hammering them with the same plug. A bent lip means altered plug motion and sometimes it's hard to notice this at night.

Secondly, I want my surface swimmers to be balanced so that they will not roll side to side in the water. I want a steady wiggle and not a roll. This requires that the plug be balanced in its construction. This is an important feature that contributes to the success of the fish catching potential of this

Some of today's most popular top water metal lip swimmers.

lure. After you have purchased the lure you should test its action under controlled conditions where you can observe its action in calm water. If the plug does not perform well in calm water then it is not likely to perform at all in rough white water. Therefore, before you buy a bunch from a single manufacturer, buy one and test it. If it does not perform well under the testing conditions, then you have just saved yourself a lot of money and now you know what brand to avoid purchasing in the future.

Thirdly, I do not want the hooks to tangle with each other on a cast or to grab the metal lip itself. Paint schemes and durability are the last considerations. It is nice to have fancy paint jobs with all sorts of colors, but let's not forget we are talking about a product made out of wood coming into contact with rocks and the teeth of gorilla bluefish. When it comes to my preference for color patterns for surface swimmers, I like light colors in the daytime as much as in the dark. White with pink stripes and herring are my favorite with yellow over white a close second. Considering half of the body of these lures is consistently out of the water I find it very hard to put too much significance on the color unless I want to impress sea gulls that are often circling above. In fact, if I could find a color pattern which these birds would not try to grab, as it is wobbling in the wave, I have a feeling it would become my favorite.

When it comes to Danny style swimmers my favorites in recent years have been those made by RM Smith, Gibbs and Beachmaster. All of these manufacturers are known for their metal lips swimmers and they all make this particular type of lure based on a design by the late Danny Pichney. In addition to the aforementioned plugs I am also partial to pikie type swimmers made by west coast builder Mike Fixter. My advice to you is to stick with a few builders whose expertise in designing metal lip swimmers you can trust. Certain builders are known for needlefish, some for their darters and others for metal lip swimmers. We can't expect one person to be great at all things so keep that in mind when planning your next purchase. I should mention that metal lip swimmers, particularly surface ones are probably the most produced type of lures on the market today and each region of the Northeast will have many local builders who turn out some very nice plugs on their lathes. Some produce them only for shows or sell them locally while others are trying to get a foothold in other areas. In either case, they make plugs that are well regarded for their quality and their swimming action. Bob Hahn, Lefty, Saltybugger, Habs, Jay1, Big Don, Woody, Garry2, and J.N-SKI are just some of builders whose surface metal lip swimmers are held in high regard on the beaches of the Northeast.

SUBSURFACE METAL LIP SWIMMERS

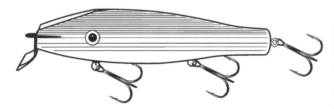

As much fun as fishing is with surface metal lip swimmers, they leave much to be desired when the fish are deep and you need to reach them. Considering fish spend most of their lives on or close to the bottom, we have to adjust our presentation in order to get our lure into their strike zone. Thinking you will coax a fish from a deep water rip to rise to the surface and slam a Danny is not just unreasonable but also very unlikely to occur. Fortunately we have at our disposal metal lip swimmers that are designed to work under the surface, some reaching depths that no other wooden lure can. When I fish in the inlets where deep boating channels are usually within close proximity to the shoreline, or around jetties and bridge abutments, the subsurface metal lip swimmer is usually my weapon of choice. I do understand and accept that in these fast moving waters, bucktails are considered the most productive lures and I do use them frequently. However, diving metal lip swimmers can do a few things that bucktails cannot. First, they offer a larger profile than the bucktail and this can often get the attention of a large fish that is not keen on chasing after small meals. Because of their slower movement through the water than bucktails, metal lip swimmers

stay in the strike zone longer, enticing game-fish with their slow wobble. If you were a fish and knowing what we know about their feeding behavior, would you be more interested in a bucktail that is in front of your face one moment and gone the next or would you be more likely to go after a big, wobbling meal that is dancing tantalizingly slow in front of your nose? I know which one I would choose. Subsurface swimmers are not just limited to

Bending the eye of the lure up will make subsurface metal lips reach their maximum depth.

deep water, they can also be used on open beaches successfully. I like to fish them in the deep troughs that are usually found between sand bars and the beach. In these locations, I often cast parallel to the beach in order to keep my swimmers in the trough as long as possible. I will bend the plug's nose wire up if I want the lure to dive deeper or down if I want it closer to surface. In rocky, shallow places like the ones found around Montauk Point, the subsurface metal lip can be very productive when cast up tide and retrieved oh-so slowly, imitating wobbling baitfish that are being carried by the current. In the inlet rips and around inlet jetties, deep diving metal lips can be absolutely deadly when retrieved as deeply as possible by bending the nose wire up as much as needed. Both of these places share a common characteristic that is very important in order to be successful with subsurface metal lip swimmers, that is, a strong current flow. Top water swimmers like the Danny for example do not excel in strong current because their "wiggle" becomes too fast and it appears unnatural. A good subsurface swimmer should have a lot less wiggle than a Danny type swimmer but more of a "roll" on its side. The flow of water washing over the plug's lip brings the best out of these plugs. When fishing deep water rips I prefer to use plugs that dig the deepest like Beachmaster Cowboys or Danny's Conrads. Most of the time, the fish will be found in the bottom third of the water column and you need to get your metal lip down there before it washes out of the rip. I find that even though I had success when working these types of plugs with spinning gear they are most effective when worked with a conventional set up. For example, the wide rips that extend themselves at a distance from the shore can be worked with conventional gear by casting far up tide and then letting line out in free spool, thumbing the line until the lure reaches the far end of the rip. Then an angler can lock the reel and begin a painfully slow retrieve back toward shore. In addition, I find that the depth a lure reaches is often crucial to my success. I find it easier to point the tip of my conventional rod into the water, while retrieving my lure, keeping my diving metal lip deeper than when I am retrieving with spinning tackle. Pointing a spinning rod at the water and retrieving it, while the butt is between your legs can be murder on one's back and you will get tired in a hurry.

With the conventional rod though, the normal retrieving position is with the rod safely tucked under your armpit. Conventional rods are also generally stiffer than their spinning counterparts and I find the added stiffness and power comes in very handy when trying to turn the fish away from barnacle covered rocks on jetties or away from a bridge abutment.

WHAT TO BUY?

When it comes to purchasing these deep diving metal lips you will find that your selection will be limited in comparison to your choices for surface swimming metal lips. Old-time wooden favorites made by Danny and

Super Strike lures have become highly sought after collectibles and unless you are willing to take out a home equity loan to acquire some, I suggest you look in other places. Tattoo's Tackle and J.N-SKI Custom Plugs make their own version of subsurface swimmers and although none of these are true deep divers they have earned reputations as proven fish catchers over the last few years. If you are looking for a truly deep diver your only choice is a Beachmaster Cowboy which unfortunately is only made sporadically. In recent years, Beachmaster Lures has made a plug they simply call "Junior". It is kind of a cross between an old Danny Pinchney Junior and a large Atom 40. This particular lure has a lot of range when it comes to depth and can be worked from very deep to just under the surface. Unlike most metal lip swimmers this particular lure has substantial weight in the tail and it can outcast any other metal lip swimmer by a wide margin. If you can find any in the stores buy one, or two or a dozen. Take them to your favorite rip, bend the nose wire up, cast it and hold on to your rod. I call it my "heat seeking missile" because if I can't get a bump on a yellow Junior, it usually means it is going to be a slow night. In fact, I cannot remember a single night where that wasn't true except for the night that the fish wanted nothing except an eel skin plug. I find subsurface metal lips to be better suited for rigging with eel skin than surface ones, mostly because the tail of the skin appears so much more alive in the

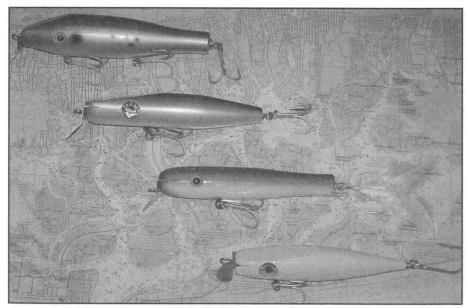

Some of today's most popular subsurface metal lip swimmers.

current under the surface than it does on top. If you are intrigued by eel skins plugs and are willing to go an extra step to procure and rig your lures, I think you will find the next chapter particularly interesting.

Subsurface metal lips, including ones fitted with eel skins do not need to be retrieved in any special way. Slow and steady, particularly when using them in swift current has always worked for me. However, when the fishing is slow or when the bait is so thick that the fish seemingly ignore every plug thrown at them, I will occasionally "sweep" my rod, to impart quick movement of the plug which mimics baitfish fleeing from a predator. Then I will allow the plug to come to rest momentarily. This technique seems to evoke strikes when nothing else is working. I know it can be absolutely maddening to think that the same retrieve will work when the fish are thick as well as when they are scarce, but it does. I guess that is why we call it fishing and not catching.

When it comes to colors I prefer darker shades on all my subsurface metal lips, except the Junior swimmer. For some reason a yellow Junior outfishes anything in my bag by a wide margin including Junior's in other patterns. Black over gold or something with a dark back and slightly lighter sides might be a good imitation of blackfish which are often found in these deep water spots. To be honest, if I had the time and unlimited financial resources, I would take the hooks off of every one of my subsurface swimmers, other than the yellow Junior, and fit all of them with eel skins. In the next chapter you will get a chance to read about two guys standing on the same rock and throwing exactly the same plug and why one catches a fish and the other does not.

TIP

Tune your metal lip swimmers in the daytime by retrieving them in calm waters and watching the action. Since each piece of wood that these lures are made out of is different, each plug should be tuned to swim to your wishes. This is the time to play with bending the lip slightly if you are not getting the desired results by bending the nose wire. Once you have done your testing it's a good idea to mark a lure in some way on the nose or the lip so you can easily identify a surface swimmer versus a diver at night. Remember, these lures can look identical in shape except the lip slot position might be higher or lower and this will greatly influence the property of the lure. If the lip slot is higher the lure will tend to dive while a middle or lower slot position will make a metal lip swimmer stay on the surface. It is difficult to compare lip slot height in the middle of the night so mark the nose with a permanent marker or a spot of paint.

CHAPTER THIRTEEN

— EEL SKIN PLUGS —

C ertain lures always have been regarded as "cow killers" because of their tendency to pull the biggest fish out of the school. In the minds of many, there are no better big fish magnets than a metal lip swimmer fitted with an eel skin. Truly large stripers are thought to be fastidiously selective eaters, choosing to feed less often than their smaller siblings but preferring larger meals. It is no wonder then that live eels take disproportionate numbers of large bass each year. Fishing with live eels however presents us with so many limitations that I personally can't accept them, so I opt for an alternative. Among my objections to using live eels are that they cast poorly and are generally useless in anything but moderate to calm wind conditions. An angler is generally limited to a specific depth in the water column unless he uses a drail or another embellishment to bring the eel towards the bottom. It also doesn't help that live eels act as bluefish magnets and that their sharp teeth reduce my eels to the size of cigar butts. There is nothing more annoying than expensive bait turned useless by toothy bluefish.

The other reason I never was enamored with the idea of using live eels, with any regularity, was the fact that these slimy little creatures will often spin around my line and make an ungodly mess as soon as I stop paying attention to them for a moment. Now, this may not be something that regularly happens to other anglers, but for me there might be some personal reason why eels feel so hostile towards me. Could it be that they know I skinned their brother and sisters in the past? Oh well, to make an omelet you have to crack a few eggs. Kidding aside, skinning an eel and slipping the skin on a metal lip plug will not just give you a deadly lure but one that is more versatile than a live one. First you can cast it further and secondly it can be worked at different depths.

Additionally, unlike live eels, plugs rigged with skins are a cinch to carry and store. I just rinse mine after each trip in cold water, toss it in a zip lock bag and into the freezer it goes.

LESSON FROM THE MASTER

My obsession with eel skin plugs started innocently enough on a fall night in a local inlet. That morning I received a phone call from my friend Bobby, maker of Beach Master lures. He told me he had crushed the fish the night before on eel skin plugs. Eel skin, shmilskin, I said to myself. Bob

has a tendency to zone in on a certain color or a particular lure and I just took it as one of those days. As the tide was not going to be dropping before 11 pm I knew my trip was going to be a short one since I had work obligations in the morning, but I just couldn't

Stripers find an eel skin plug irresistible and often attack it with much more determination than they do live eels.

stay home. We drove to the inlet and after we suited up he handed me a redesigned Beachmaster Junior already fitted with an eel skin. I looked at the monstrosity for a moment but then quickly stuffed it into my bag with no intention of using it. Once we got close to the shore it was evident that there was a lot of life in the surf as peanut bunker were being ambushed by stripers and were leaping out of the water. Excitedly, I cast a diving metal lip up current and started the retrieve but the only thing I managed to "catch" were a few peanut bunker that were snagged in their backs. I went through my plugs much faster than usual as I knew I had limited time to fish since the current was slowing down.

Bobby was standing about 20 yards away, with his conventional stick pointing at the water. A passerby would never know what was transpiring until a large bass started thrashing in the shallow water in front of him. Bob bent down and grabbed it by the jaw and quickly released it without turning on his light. He nailed about a dozen fish in an hour while I was still looking for my first bump. Suddenly he jumped off his rock and walked past me heading toward his buggy. He put his lift gate down and cracked a beer. I was perplexed as to what was going on when suddenly I saw three anglers appear as they just stepped out from the darkness. After exchanging pleasantries, they decided to make a few casts in the vicinity but soon found out that although there was a lot of bait, the fish

were few and far between. After about half an hour they left and Bobby hurriedly walked past me and back to his rock. Only then did I realize that in fear of giving up the action, he had in front of him, he stopped fishing and walked away. Soon after he made his first cast as I looked up and believe it or not he was once again into a fish. At this point I went through every plug in my bag, except for that ugly looking eel skin plug. Since my confidence was nonexistent at this point I figured I had nothing to lose and I tied it on. I made a cast up-tide and started a retrieve, not exactly sure what retrieve to use with the contraption that was attached to my

In the hand of a seasoned angler the eel skin plug becomes a deadly weapon.

leader. Just as I was thinking about the retrieve, my lure got slammed and my rod doubled over under the strain of a good fish.

I'd love to tell you that I hammered the fish from this point on but the truth was, shortly afterwards I had to split in order to get a few hours of shuteye before going to work. I asked Bobby why in his opinion the eel skin plug that he was using was so effective yet every other plug failed to elicit a strike. He told me that expecting my peanut bunker imitation to be noticed among thousands of real things in the water is unreasonable. Something large, that can wiggle slowly in the strike zone will usually draw some interest from the fish. I still wasn't convinced. Intrigued, yes but not totally convinced.

STUDENT BECOMES A TEACHER

A few weeks later Bobby left for a NASCAR race in Texas and I decided to try another spot in an inlet that was closer to home. It was two days before a full November moon and the conditions on this particular night had all the makings of a disappointing trip. The night was clear and the moon was too bright for my liking but the season was slipping away. There would be plenty of time to sleep in the winter, I told myself as I walked deep into the inlet.

My plan was to start on the backside of the inlet seawall and work my way towards the mouth of it as the tide dropped. The area I was headed towards is littered with rocks from the remains of a jetty that long ago collapsed into the ocean. I was hoping to intercept fish looking for a meal around these small rocks. At this spot there is also one large boulder that remains where the old jetty use to be. It protrudes above the water about twenty yards from the shore and a nice rip forms around it. I have done well here over the years with lots of action but never really managed to get any quality fish. As I was settling onto the rocks I could hear small splashes around the big boulder, welcome evidence of some life in the water.

I started with a 1 ounce bucktail casting it up tide from the rock and letting it naturally float in the current. However, it failed to evoke a bump. A few casts later I decided that although the presence of fish was clearly evident it wasn't the bucktail that they wanted. Unfortunately the mix of metal lips and darters I threw suffered the same fate as the bucktail. I leaned back onto the rock in frustration and gazed at the starry sky.

As I was catching my breath, I thought about my experience with Bobby a few weeks earlier. I opened my bag and grudgingly pulled out an eel skin Junior swimmer, almost repulsed by it as it glistened in the moonlight. I figured since the fish were not cooperating, at least I could look into the bright moonlit water and observe how the lure looked and worked during the retrieve. Standing high on the rock above the rip gave me a nice birds-eye view of the lure. Sure enough, the junior wobbled around the big boulder without a sniff but regardless I admired the beautiful wiggle of the trailing eel skin tail. The plug was about a rod length away from the base of the rock, when I lowered my tip getting ready to lift it out of the water. A large shadow appeared behind it, opened its cavernous mouth and engulfed it. The sharp hooks quickly found their mark and the striper, now realizing what just happened started thrashing its tail on the surface. I was half stunned, half paralyzed by fear that the tension and close proximity of the fish would cause the hooks to pull out and the plug would end up flying into my face.

Fortunately, the striper managed to turn on its side and headed towards the deep water channel. I let out a sigh of relief but it did not last long as the fish changed direction, heading straight for the big boulder. I knew that if it managed to reach that rock I was going to be on the losing end of this battle as the barnacle crusted rock had cost me fish before. I tightened up on the drag and engaged in a battle of wills with the fish. Either the hooks were going to tear out or the line was going to snap but I wasn't about to let it reach that boulder. For a moment the time seemed to stand still with two adversaries giving it their all when I sensed that the striper was giving up in its quest and was now starting to turn towards me. Within moments I slid the fish on the rock, a thirty pound striper was illuminated by the moon. Quickly released, I watched it slowly make its way toward the boulder until it disappeared from sight.

I checked my snap and made another cast, not expecting anything but knowing my night was already made. I could feel my eel skin wobbling in the rip when it got slammed with authority and the drag started to sing with line peeling off the reel. Considering I had tightened my drag on the previous fish, I was alarmed by the rate line was coming off the reel. The fish headed into the current fighting both my drag and the water flow. This

Although effective on oceanfront beaches eel skin plugs really shine around rock piles, jetties and inlet rips.

proved to be too much for the fish and I could sense, from the bend in my rod, that it was getting more tired after each run. Finally it gave up completely and I managed to get my hand into its jaw. I was stunned that this fish was even larger than the one before, especially considering that this spot had never given up a twenty pound fish, never mind a fish almost twice that size. Within the next hour I landed another few fish and lost at least that many all between twenty and thirty pounds.

The following night I wanted to share my experience with a friend, so I took my buddy Rob with me to the same spot. As luck would have it we were very disappointed to find only a lone schoolie in that spot. I suggested we make a move a few hundred yards towards the inlet jetty. I knew from experience that at the end of the tide a nice rip sets up at the tip of the jetty. I just had to prove to Rob that the eel skin plug worked. Rob drew first blood by raising a fish but failed to get a solid hook up. An hour later without a touch, I moved away from the tip and towards mid jetty. I wanted to angle my cast into the pocket by casting back toward the shore where the jetty met the sand. My idea was to work the eel skin plug parallel to the rocks towards the rip instead of working the rip. However, I put too much into my cast and my eel skin plug landed on the dry sand. I sheepishly reeled and dragged it into the water while Rob stood at the jetty tip with a big smile on his face. Just as he was about to comment on my casting skills, the water exploded at the lip of the beach with splashing and a huge commotion. To our surprise it was a bass that must have been lying in water that was inches deep and not more than three feet from dry sand. Now that it had attacked my plug it was flapping uncontrollably because it could not swim away.

Finally, after several tail slaps it was able to make a turn away from the beach and it headed for deeper water between the two jetties. Rob stood on his rock with a puzzled look on his face, and his grin now turned into amazement. After landing the fish I released it quickly and made another cast into the same area. It did not take long for another bass to find the eel skin plug and once again in the shallow water it started crashing the surface as the hooks found their mark. At this time it was obvious to me that Rob was getting annoyed, so I called him over and instructed him to cast in the same location. He threw the same Beachmaster junior that I did, except his did not have an eel skin on it. In the next six casts I landed six fish, all over twenty pounds while he did not even get a bump.

Rumor has it that Rob skipped church the next morning and was seen nervously pacing in front of the local eel supplier waiting for him to open the doors. True or not, I don't think either one of us will look at eel skin plugs the same way again. In addition to metal lip swimmers there is another lure that is a great candidate for fitting with eel skin. Needlefish lures are great fish producers in their own right but they become absolutely deadly when fitted with an eel skin. Work them the same way you would a regular needlefish, either straight or with intermittent, light jerks of the rod. In either scenario keep the retrieve as slow as possible.

RIGGING AN EEL SKIN METAL LIP SWIMMER

One should not be intimidated by the process of fitting an eel skin on a metal lip swimmer. First you must decide which plug you will use for the job at hand. My preference lies with subsurface swimmers but Danny style swimmers are also great candidates to be fitted with a skin. Stay away from pikies or surfsters as they are designed to swim with their heads angled downward and the tail in the air, slapping at the water. You will kill the action of these plugs if you fit them with a skin because of the way they were designed.

I would also suggest that you pick a plug that you have a high degree of confidence in because a lousy plug with the skin on it is still a lousy plug, only uglier. First you will need a whole dead eel of approximately the same circumference behind the anal vent as the lure you intend to put it on.

Another way to approximately judge the size of an eel is for a useable skin to be twice as long as the lure it will be fitted on. Needless to say, you will need very large eels to be usable for rigging. Rub a dead eel with kosher salt and then with paper towels, remove as much slime from its body as possible. Next, nail the eel through its head to a fence post or board and with a razor blade make a small incision around the body just below the gills. With two pair of pliers, one on each side of the eel, start pulling downward on the skin until the skin starts to peel off the body. Once you get around the anal vent pay close attention that the eel's flesh does not start to tear and come off with the skin. Once you are past this point the rest of the skin should peel easily and come off in one piece.

Now if any flesh is attached to the skin it should be removed with a dull object like a spoon or a clam knife. I only use the skin below the vent as the hole in the anal vent often tears during the rigging process. At this point I would cut the skin above the anal vent and discard it. In order to

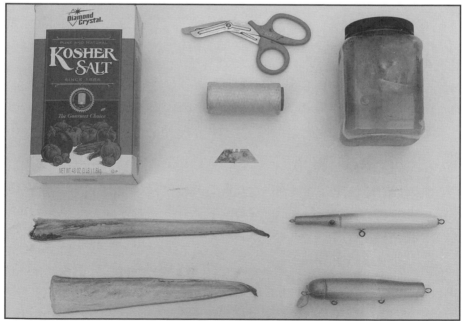

To make the rigging process as simple as possible have everything you need on hand before skinning an eel.

toughen up the skin make a solution of equal parts water and kosher salt. Bring it to a boil and let all salt dissolve then cool it completely. This should be done the day before you are skinning eels.

Next soak the skin in the cold brine for at least a day, preferably two. You can keep the brine and the extra skins in your freezer indefinitely and the salt will prevent the water from completely freezing. In the mean time prepare your metal lip swimmer by removing all hooks. Before you go through the

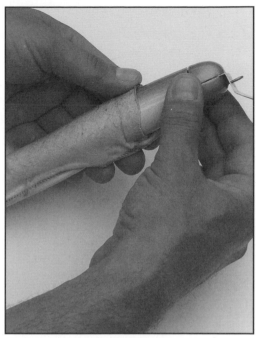

Sliding a skin over the lure.

actual process of sliding the skin onto the plug you must decide to either leave the skin inverted or reverse to its natural dark color. For me this is a no brainier as I always rig my plug with the inverted side. The blue hue of the inverted skin resembles many of the baitfish that reside in our waters. Besides I have had the most success with the plug rigged this way.

The time tested method is to slide a skin with the darker side of the inverted (blue) skin on top of the plug while making sure the eel skin seams run along the top and on the belly right over the swivel, just like they do on real eels. After rinsing the skin in cold water slide it over the back of the lure and work it up slowly toward the front, paying close attention to the place where the swivel protrudes through the lure. Applying too much pressure at this point can tear a hole in the skin. Essentially you are putting the skin on your plug in the same way you pull your sock over your foot. Work the skin up over the plug towards the metal lip until there are about two to three inches of skin hanging behind the plug. I like my skin to extend two to three inches behind the lure. If you go longer than this you are inviting the possibility of the skin catching the hooks during a cast. In addition, the longer the skin on the back, the larger the lure will appear

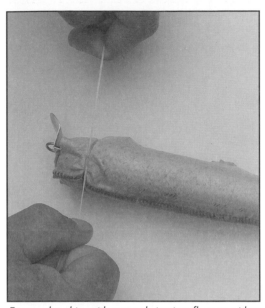

Fasten the skin with waxed rigging floss to either the groove in the plug or around the metal lip.

and considering the hook is usually situated towards the front of the plug, this might result in a lot of short hits when fish will hit the plug but miss the hook. Having said that, many old-timers use a skin about twice as long as the lure and leave a tail much longer than two to three inches. I'll leave this up to you. You can make them in a few different configurations and see which one you prefer based on casting distance and desired action they might produce.

Once the skin is set where you want it, making sure the eel seam run straight over the belly and right on top of the swivel. Take some waxed rigging floss or Dacron and secure the skin to the plug by tying an overhand square knot at the point were the metal lip meets the wood. If your plug is designed for the use of an eel skin it will be equipped with a groove a little bit behind the front of the plug. Fasten it right on the groove with your knot on the belly. Now turn

With a razor cut the smallest possible hole and work the swivel through it. To reduce possible tearing make sure the cut is perpendicular to the seam on the eel skin.

the plug over and do another square knot on the top before flipping the plug over to its original position and tying another set of square knots. The nice part about working with waxed rigging floss is that it "bites" into itself during the knot making process, holding the pressure while you tie a square knot over it. Finish it by trimming the floss or Dacron close to the knot and apply a drop of Zap-a-gap or other fast drying glue on the knot.

Some anglers like to trim the excess skin as close as possible to the threads but I think there is a better way. I like to trim my skin about half an inch in front of the thread and then fold it back over the thread. Doing it this way the threads are hidden under the skin making for a much better presentation. Use a razor blade to make a tiny incision at the point where the swivel is located. Always make a cut with a razor blade perpendicular to the eel spine which runs along the length of the plug. If you cut a skin in the same direction the skin seam is running you are taking a chance that the skin will tear completely over time along the seam. Now work the swivel through the tiny hole in the skin. Finally, attach you favorite hook and go get that striper cow of your dreams.

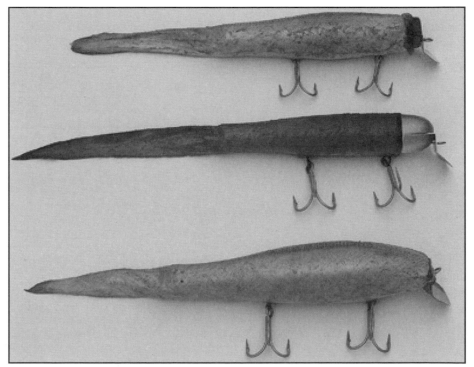

Rigging eel skins on different types of metal lip swimmers allow us to use them at different depths in the water column.

TIP

If a straight retrieve is not producing the desired results, try sweeping the eel skin forward with a long sweep of the rod. Let it rest for a moment while you pick up the slack then do it again. This little trick will often entice even the most uncooperative fish.

CHAPTER FOURTEEN

— PLASTIC SWIMMERS —

Chances are that Bomber, Cotton Cordell, Rebel or Yo-Zuri made the first lure you ever purchased. These plastic swimmers are affordable, virtually indestructible, come in more colors than any other type of lure and most important, they catch a ton of fish with just a simple straight retrieve. It is not surprising then that these swimmers are the most recommended lures to those who are just joining our ranks. Before the 1960's, plastic swimmers were relegated primarily for use in fresh water. Small hooks, weak split rings and brittle plastic bodies stood no chance of holding up to the brute strength of a striper or the harsh saltwater environment. After some anglers modified their lures for use in the surf and racked up impressive catches, some manufacturers sensed the opportunity to expand their products into the saltwater fishing market. Some just added better components to their existing products. They changed the split rings or hooks while others made their plugs larger to satisfy those who were calling for bigger baitfish imitations. However, let's be honest, even small plugs with better hooks are still, to this day, no match for a decent fish unless the angler opts to use a very light drag setting.

One of my all-time favorite lures is a small 4-inch sinking Rebel. I often fish this plug just suspended in the current with an occasional twitch. One night I found fish stacked up at the mouth of a back bay creek waiting eagerly for the dropping tide to flush out the small baitfish that were hiding in the marshes. I lost count of how many stripers I had this night but the thing that stuck in my mind was that even though I was using a light nine foot rod, most of the fish managed to straighten out or bend the hooks even with a light drag. These weren't big fish by any means; mostly teen size stripers but the fact that I used braid in conjunction with a fast current caused the hooks to open. After I landed each fish, I painstakingly bent the hooks back into shape. This went on all night long and to this day I am reluctant to toss a plastic swimmer less than 4 inches long into a pod of fish.

You can only upgrade the size and the strength of your hooks to a certain extent. After that the hook weight or its size will start to affect the swimming motion of a plug and nine out of ten times this is not a good

This striper engulfed a Bomber in the dark.

thing. I am much more comfortable with 5 or 7 inch models than I am with smaller ones primarily because I can use strong saltwater hooks without affecting the action of the lure itself. These lures can be divided into two categories, sinking or suspending models and floating or surface ones. For a long time, the most popular surface swimmer has been a 7 inch Redfin. Its seductive wiggle on the surface has fooled so many bass and bluefish over the years that most sharpies I know consider it a "must have lure." On the other hand, most subsurface models are retrieved between one and six feet in depth and feature a plastic lip, which gives them all the action they need. Bomber lures are the leaders in this category and one of the lures that dig the deepest. Rebel, Yo-Zuri and many other companies make similar "minnow" style lures in a wide array of lengths and weights. In addition some companies, like Yo-Zuri, have added magnetic weights in the belly of their lures, which shift the weight of the lure backwards on each cast aiding in casting distance. While on the subject of casting distance, I would be remiss if I didn't mention that many surfcasters today want to cast a mile regardless of the structure they are presenting their lures to. It's a type of manly macho thing where every cast should be placed as far from the shore as possible with very little regard to where the fish are actually located. For this reason many anglers today frown on using these lures as they perceive them as poor casters. But these same anglers then proceed to fill their bags with metal lip swimmers, which in all honesty are even worse casters than plastic swimmers.

Most of the action is taking place close to the shore, between the sand bar and the beach. That's where the fish usually are. And this area is well within the range of these lures. In fact, these lures become even more effective when used in conjunction with a teaser, something that will cut the casting distance even further. They are one of the few lures I use in tandem with teasers. Early in the spring I like to use small 4 to 5 inch models, as I take into account the fact that most of the fish I will catch will be of a smaller size and they will be feeding on tiny bait. During this time the water temperatures are still very cold and fish can be quite sluggish in their feeding habits. Hits are usually light and at times barely noticeable. When I sense that fish are feeding in this manner I follow the advice of my friend and one of the most astute students of the sport, New York surf guide Bill Wetzel. He recommends breaking the retrieve sequence by gently either rolling the rod in his palm, tipping the rod lightly or changing retrieve

Big bass have always found the wiggle of Redfin's irresistible to pass up.

speeds. This seems to work much better than a straight retrieve when the fish are sluggish. I don't usually stay with these small swimming plugs for more than a week or two as I start searching for bigger fish as soon as some larger baitfish arrive in the area.

My favorite plugs for year round use are Bombers and Redfin's. I don't like to carry more than a few plastic swimmers in my bag and I feel that with these two plugs I can cover a lot of water: the surface with Redfins and the subsurface with Bombers. When it comes to size the six-inch Bomber is almost always included in my bag with the larger 17A version used sparingly in the fall. I don't particularly care for the jointed version as they cast poorly and vibrate under the surface way too much for my liking. Yellow again is my "go-to" color with anything blue or green on the back a second choice. You might have heard about "chicken scratch" or "school bus" patterns as colors which you "must have" in order to catch fish. I tried them for a few years and found them to be inferior to plain yellow. For what it is worth, they have been hanging in my garage ever since. It's one of those colors that worked so well at one point in time that it garnered an almost cult like following. Of course, when everyone and their mother end up casting a single color, it is kind of hard to draw conclusions about its efficacy since there are no other colors to compare it to. I still insist it's the presentation and size of the lure that will have the greatest influence on one's success and not the choice of a color. The nice part about using these plugs is that all the action is caused by the plastic lip so your job is simply to control the speed of their movement through the water. The best advice I can give you is to retrieve these plugs crawlingly slow and when you think you are going too slow, then slow down some more, particularly at night. These plugs are designed to swim almost suspended in the water column and they are most effective when using a slow retrieve. When it comes to the Redfin, I prefer the 7-inch model for year round use. I don't use it in the spring because where I fish there rarely is any top water action taking place early in the year. The 5-inch model although it swims very appealing is difficult to cast with even a light breeze. Not that the seven-inch model is a great caster but it's much better than its smaller version. In late spring, when fish become more active, the Redfin becomes very effective in the surf, especially at night casting behind the curl of the wave. Later in the summer, the chrome Redfin becomes almost a fish magnet as predators often mistake it for snapper bluefish struggling on the surface. Then in the fall it becomes a steady producer particularly in locations where metal lip swimmers are also effective.

During stormy periods and consequent rough water conditions the plug has a tendency to roll out of the wave and become unproductive. For this reason many sharpies resort to loading their Redfin with water to make them more stable. A word of caution. In my experience, as limited as it might be compared to some who have done this for years, a Redfin should be loaded only enough to improve its stability in rough water while keeping its signature wiggle. This plug was never meant to be and it never will be a great casting plug regardless of how much weight you add to it. But you might do more damage than good by overloading it with water and effecting its action. By adding the right amount of weight, the balance and the pivot point of the lure should remain intact, the wobbling action should remain the same or even improve and it should hold better in the rough water. If you still want your plug to cast further, grab a pencil popper.

LOADING A REDFIN

Loading a 7-inch Redfin can be done either at home or if desired, right on the beach. The method described below deals with a quick and effective beach modification. For this project you will need a pair of pliers, a thin nail and a syringe, preferably one that holds 10cc or more of water. Hold the nail with the pliers and heat up its tip with a cigarette lighter or a candle. Once the nail has gotten hot insert it at once through the plastic body of the Redfin making sure you don't penetrate the body on the other side. This can also be done easily with a drill and a thin drill bit if you are doing it at home. The insertion could be made anywhere on the top portion of the lure from the hook hanger to the head but not through the seam where the Redfin is joined .The Redfin is made out of two half's and joining seam runs along the top of the lure and on its belly. Now insert the syringe into the hole and fill the cavity with 10cc of water. I have heard of guys using bunker oil instead of water and then filling the hole with a sponge so that bunker oil can be slowly released behind the plug, creating a natural "chum" line. All I can say is that I don't want to be the guy who has to open the lure bag where this contraption has been stored for a few days in the hot sun because the stench would be incredible. After you put the water into the chamber, re-heat the nail. Once it is very hot, use it to smear the plastic around the hole. Push the melted plastic into the opening thus closing up the hole. If you want to get real-ly fancy you can break off a toothpick in the hole and then use epoxy to fill the hole.

Use a drill or a hot nail to penetrate through the plastic body.

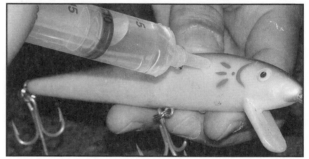

Load the Redfin with 10cc of water and seal the hole.

TIP

If you are really feeling adventurous you might try modifying the plastic lip on these plugs by slowly heating the lip with a low flame. After the lip has softened, bend it slightly downwards and then let it cool. This will increase the wiggle of the lure substantially with the most pronounced action visible on Redfins that you work on the surface. I have played with this modification in the past I find that it works best in a calm surf or back bay waters. In the rough surf it will tend to dig into the wave and twitch uncontrollably providing too much wiggle.

CHAPTER FIFTEEN

— BUCKTAILS & SOFT PLASTIC BAITS —

What do you get when you combine a piece of lead, a handful of hair from the tail of a deer, a plain hook and a slice of pork skin? How about the best darn fishing lure ever known to man! It's kind of ironic that we trip over each other trying to buy the latest and greatest hot lure with gorgeous paint jobs when Navy Seals include a lowly bucktail in their survival kit. Why do they do it? Without a doubt it is because bucktails catch more fish, in more locations, with more consistency than any other lure. Why are bucktails so effective from inshore waters to the offshore canyons and everywhere in between? I would have to say the answer is versatility. They can be worked deep in inlet rips, bounced over rocky bottoms, cast into the strongest in-your-face winds, float them in still water or my favorite, work them through big sets of white water on open sand beaches. A very bright fisherman once commented, "They imitate nothing but look like everything". That is so true! I guess the closest thing you could compare them to would be a pulsating squid, but even that is a stretch. Bucktails move with the flutter that has always been impossible for fish to pass up.

If these lures are so effective why don't surfcasters toss their wood in the fireplace and fill their bags with nothing but bucktails? The truth is some anglers have done just that. A few Montauk locals, considered by many to be among the hardest working surfcasters on the east coast, carry nothing but a half a dozen bucktails in their pocket and they catch hundreds and hundreds of stripers, bluefish and weakfish each year. As much as Montauk regulars might love tossing darters in the middle of the night, few would ever venture on a daytime expedition without their beloved buck-tails. The same could be said for the jetty jocks that often heave heavy bucktails off the rock piles that border inlets or the anglers that use more of a finesse approach in the back bays.

When I fish the sandy oceanfront beaches I am looking for similar con-ditions as I do when I fish most plugs: a wind in my face and plenty of white water. The difference is with bucktails is that there never is "too much" wind. Strong onshore winds mean bigger waves that result in the water column expanding vertically by as much as a few feet. This also means we can now work heavier bucktails as we have plenty of water to work them in. Of course, bigger bucktails cast well into a strong wind and that is why I said; there is never too much wind for using a bucktail.

Most of the time we have moderate surf conditions and bucktails from a 1/2 to 1 ounces should suffice along gradually sloping sandy beaches. Again, I prefer some wave action on the ocean instead of calm conditions, more so with bucktails and metal lip swimmers than any other lures. Since previously in this book, I have gone into detail about the importance of white water, I will not bore you with any more advice other than to stress keeping that bucktail behind the wave as long as possible. That and mak-ing sure your bucktails always land behind a cresting wave during a cast.

Bucktails truly are a lure that the angler needs to have a "feel" for during the retrieve regardless of which location or type of structure he is target-ing. A bucktail should almost become an extension of your arm because ever-small twitches of your wrist will become an exag-gerated motion under water.

Bucktails are most productive in white water conditions or when used in an area with good current flow.

SIZE THEM UP

Picking the right size bucktail will have an important influence on your fishing success. Therefore, it pays to take a few minutes to figure out what size to use. Here I mean the weight of the bucktail. The size is dictated by the conditions and location you plan to fish. What I like to do is to make a cast and start a slow and straight retrieve. If my bucktail touches the bottom I will go a size lighter until I find the size that is not dragging in the sand. I will try to work the bucktail as deep as possible without consistently hitting the bottom. As ocean bottoms are irregular in shape, an occasional scrape is acceptable and at times even desirable. However, when you start plowing the sand during the retrieve the lead head looses its effectiveness.

Once I settle on the size of the bucktail, I like to employ a small twitch during my retrieve instead of just a straight one. The important point though is not to overdo the twitching part because you are very likely to pull the bucktail away from the fish just as it's getting ready

Uncle Josh pork rinds are a staple of Northeast bucktailers.

to strike. The twitching should be done with a quick flick of the wrist instead of moving the rod in a big arc or sweep. This latter motion tends to move the bucktail away from the bottom and out of the strike zone. Not using the sweeping action has recently become even more important with the popularity of braided lines, as even a small movement with the rod is exaggerated. This happens under the waters surface because braid has very little stretch and every small motion is quickly and effectively transmitted to the lure.

When faced with calm conditions on open beaches or when working the shallow waters of protected bays or estuaries, I would suggest, "floating" a bucktail. Instead of using tiny bucktails in order to keep them off the bottom, I would rather use a heavier bucktail with an embellishment like an Uncle Josh Porker rind trailer or a large plastic grub. These adornments will keep the bucktail from sinking too fast. My reasoning for this is that heavier bucktails can be cast further than the lighter sizes. In addition, I like to use "thick" bucktails, ones made with an abundance of hair around the hook. The benefit of using these types of bucktails is that their hair density slows their rate of descent to the bottom. For example, if you are fishing a rocky shallow area, such as around Montauk Point, you know from experience that bucktails from 3/4 to 1 ounce are deadly here. However, with a strong wind in your face you will not be able to reach the fish with these light bucktails. Instead you could substitute a denser 1-1/2 ounce bucktail and increase your casting distance dramatically as compared to the 1 ounce version. If the bucktail has a lot more hair or you are using it with a trailer you will find that it sinks a lot slower.

In contrast, if you are fishing fast, deep water you want your bucktail to sink faster. Therefore, you want a bucktail with more weight and less hair. The inlet jetty jocks often fish their bucktails deep in the water column. Because of strong currents in these areas, they do not have the luxury of time to get down deep. Sparser bucktails will get to the bottom faster than dense ones. Speaking of jetty jocks, these highly specialized anglers often use different gear than an oceanfront angler. Because their bucktails often range from 1-1/2 ounces during slack water to as much as 5 ounces when current is cranking at full force, stiffer rods are needed to carry the extra payload. Conventional rods are much better suited for this task than spinning setups, as they make it easier to control the bucktail. When you start talking about any lead head or for that matter any lure that weighs over 5 ounces, it might be a weight that is unimaginable for you and where you fish. However, in places such as the Cape Cod Canal they are just another lure and the conventional set-up is the only way to go in order to present these heavy lures to their maximum potential. This is not just true for bucktails but also for lures like giant pikies, large deep diving metal lip swimmers, rigged eels and those massive rubber shads.

PRESENTATION

I feel that the presentation of a bucktail is more critical than when using a wooden or plastic lure. The reason for my opinion is that they do not look like anything. A straight retrieve advocated by some experts is great if you are just starting and are looking to gain some confidence and get a feel for the lure. The angler who has gotten past this point should be thinking about how his lure appears in relation to the structure he is fishing.

Personally, I like to use bucktails in conjunction with two things, current and white water. Lack of either one and you can be assured that the bucktails are not leaving the confines of my bag. I already went over the way I fish my bucktails in white water. Deep water strategies are very different. In places where the water is fast and deep, most of the fish will be holding close to the bottom. There might be some smaller and more aggressive fish higher in the water column but the big girls will almost always position themselves close to the bottom. Most of us assume, when fishing these places, that the bottom is flat. We often wonder if the fish are constantly moving through the rip or are they stationary. It could be both but they

Giant weakfish like their bucktails as much as their smaller siblings.

do not need much bottom structure to turn it into a resting place and an ambush location. If there is a small indentation in the ocean floor, even just large enough to hold a single fish, a bass can lie there without feeling the effects of the current above its head. The same can be said for a boulder that will divert current flow around itself and provide an eddy in the back of itself where a fish can rest. When you think about these obstructions, hiding holes or other irregularities that fish might use to their advantage they all share one common characteristic, they are all on or close to the bottom. Guess where we should be retrieving our bucktail? That's right; in exactly the same spots. Picking the correct size bucktail that will sink to the bottom before it reaches these areas is critical. If the bucktail is too light for the task it will zoom right over the fish's head. The easiest way to accomplish this is with a conventional rod by casting up tide and letting the bucktail hit the bottom. Once you feel the slack in your line, you start reeling with a slight twitch but only for a few turns. If you don't get a hit you free spool the reel until the bucktail hits the bottom again and repeat the process. This retrieve will assure that you are always on or close to bottom and your bucktail is in the strike zone. Of course this type of retrieve is a lot more manageable with a conventional set-up than with a spinning outfit. However, the spinning crowd has some advantages too. I occasionally decide to leave my conventional stick at home if I plan to fish the whole duration of a tide. At slack or slow moving water I often like to use light bucktails and small swimming plugs and I find the task of doing so with conventional gear too cumbersome especially if the wind is in my face. In addition, casting a light bucktail is a lot more manageable with a spinning rod than a conventional one.

Adding a strip of either Uncle Josh 240S or 70S pork rind to a bucktail makes this lure really come to life.

BUCKTAIL TRAILERS

Regardless if I am using a tiny 3\8 ounce bucktail in the back bays while I am hunting for weakfish or a 4 ounce one in a deep rip, I always use some kind of hook embellishment in conjunction with my lead head. I am a huge fan of Uncle Josh products and most of the time you will find me with a pork rind attached to the hook of my bucktail. Years ago we all used nothing but rinds that were white on both sides but these days we have many choices in this category. I prefer red over white pattern as every baitfish that swims in our water has a dark back and light belly. In order to make full use of this pattern you must impale your pork rind with the white side down so that the red side will be on top during the retrieve. Using a bucktail without some sort of embellishment is like kissing your sister. You could do it, but why? Yes, you may catch a few fish on plain bucktails but then again even a blind squirrel finds a nut once in a while. Adding a trailer to the bucktail hook may be the reason why bucktails are so productive. First and probably most important, a trailer adds the appearance of life to the bucktail due to the fluttering action behind the hook. This is akin to a baitfish moving its tail. Second, it elongates the size of the bucktail making it appear much longer than it actually is and lastly, its buoyancy can be used to slow the rate of descent of the lure.

A properly cared for pork rind can last for years and can be used again and again. It even offers some degree of resistance against the razor sharp teeth of a bluefish. The only downside to using the pork rind is that it creates a lot of wind resistance when used in very windy conditions. To combat this you can split the pork rind in half lengthwise and then make a slit in the wider side in order to give the rind its signature wiggle. You'll end up with a trailer that casts better in the wind yet it will still produce the flutter. Using a pork rind modified in this manner is also very effective when trying to present a long and slender profile. Early in the spring and late fall when sand eels are a mainstay of a striper's diet, bucktails with thin and fluttering pork rind become one of the most productive lures in the surf. I am partial to the Uncle Josh model 240S and this is what I use most of the time although I will use #70-S when I am trying to increase the profile of my presentation. However, you can't go wrong by following the advice of one of the most respected anglers on the east coast, Bill "Doc" Muller. He advises matching the length of the pork rind to the length of the bucktail, for example a 3/4 ounce bucktail with a 3-inch rind, a 1 ounce with 4-inch rind and a 1-1/4 with a 5-inch pork rind. "Doc" as he is affectionately known in surfcasting circles is an astute student of the sport and has written many books and articles about the sport he dearly loves. His recent book "Ultimate Guide to Fishing with Bucktails" should be required reading for anyone looking to become more proficient fishing bucktails.

Many anglers use twister tails or similar plastic trailers instead of pork rind and some in fact claim that they are more productive than pork rind. I tend to take this with a grain of salt as I have done some experimenting with plastic trailers and found them to be inferior to pork rind. I find that if the retrieve is a little fast the twister or grubs tend to straighten out and stop fluttering at all. If the retrieve is painfully slow I find that they don't flutter at all and come through the water almost motionless. Of course, let's not forget that one chomp from a bluefish and you are out of business. Don't get me wrong, they have their moments but just don't expect me to leave my pork rinds at home.

If I do use a plastic embellishment in conjunction with a bucktail it will most likely be a jelly worm. Mann's 10-inch strawberry jelly worms have been my favorites for many years particularly when I am looking for weakfish during the summer months. Threading one on a small bucktail or even on just a plain leadhead has been by far the most productive strategy for me. I like to match the weight of my leadhead to the speed of the current so that all I have to do is twitch my jelly worm as it is floating by. I find strawberry red to be the most productive color but I also have done well with bubble gum. If you have a hard time finding the bubble gum color just mix some strawberry red and white jelly worms in a Ziploc bag. Shake the bag and mix the worms for a few days and eventually the white worms will turn pink. Pink has always worked well with weakfish.

DO COLORS MATTER?

I don't spend much time picking a color pattern for my bucktails as I use white about 95% of the time. I have yet to find a color combination that is more productive than plain white in daytime and even in the hours of darkness. As I indicate in the previous paragraph, I do like red, strawberry or pink when I am strictly concentrating on weakfish. I find that weakfish, at times, will ignore certain color but almost never one with a flash of red. I have experienced some success with dark colored bucktails in the past. However; I have yet to see any benefit of using black or purple instead of white. In contrast, in stained and dirty water after a storm, high visibility colors such as green and yellow, also called parrot, are a must. These colors stand out much more than white does. Then again, dirty water is not exactly something that gets me drooling either. There is one more important thing I want to mention. Regardless of what brand of bucktail you use, insist on very strong, big hooks. Some of the newer brands that have hit the market in recent years have extra sharp hooks but they are made out of thin wire and I've seen these hooks bend and even break under the weight of a small fish.

Bucktailer extraordinaire Vito Orlando fishes white bucktails almost exclusively.

I prefer Andrus bucktails for just about every application except for targeting weakfish. For this type of fishing, Blue Frog bucktails are my favorites. They offer a large selection of head types and have many with reddish hair patterns. In addition, their swing hook design removes the leverage the fish can put on the bucktail, always a plus when targeting these beautiful fish that have weak membranes in their mouths. There are dozens of other brands on the market not including those tied by your friendly, neighborhood tackle shops and you know what ?They all catch fish. I am just used to the two aforementioned brands; I know their hooks and have a lot of confidence in them. Lately, my good friend Al Albano has been tying extra dense bucktails for me, with a lot of pink flash in the hair. I call them "Liberace" as they are absolutely stunning. He uses an extra long red feather that acts in a similar way that pork rind does when in the water. We did very well with these lures over the last few years with no additional embellishments. Of course, one sniff from your friendly neighborhood bluefish and all the painstaking work of tying these lures is lost.

PLASTIC SOFT BAITS

There are many rubber trailers on the market today that can be used in conjunction with  bucktails and lead heads. Slug-Go, Surf Hog, RonZ, Fin-S and Hogy's are probably the most popular ones but there are literally hundreds of other choices available. I find that most of these soft baits are much more productive when used in conjunction with plain lead heads than they are with bucktails. Slug-go rubber baits have become extremely popular in recent years and have accounted for some impressive striped bass catches. I often fish them just by impaling them on a long shank lead head and twitching them slightly on the retrieve. Another rigging method developed by Steve McKenna has captured the imagination of surf and boat anglers in recent years. As one of Rhode Island's best surfcasters, Steve's clear and concise writing about this method coupled with his many notable catches of big stripers has made the double rigging system the most prevalent way to rig a big Slug-go. It has become so popular in fact that many new manufacturers have entered the mar-

Surfcasters today have a large variety of rubber baits and trailers to choose from.

ket with their products already pre-rigged and ready to use out of the package. Surf Hog and Hogy are two leading manufacturers which have made their products available pre-rigged and ready to fish right out of the package.

Although it seems there are lots of different ways these lures can be retrieved, I find that for me, two have worked better than any others. One retrieve requires the angler to work a lure similar to a pencil popper with a steady whipping motion of the rod while the Slug-go is dancing on the surface. I find this type of retrieve to work best with longer parabolic rods especially when used in conjunction with the white water strategy I outlined in this book. The second retrieve works better with shorter rods in the eight or nine foot category. These rod lengths also facilitate using this method when standing on a rock, jetty or any place above the water level. The important thing here is to keep the Slug-go, or another similar lure, below the surface at all times as the ratio of strikes dramatically increases when the lure is kept under the surface. I like to retrieve these lures with rods pointing to the side instead of in front of me and twitching the bait intermittently. Honestly though, there really is no wrong way to retrieve these lures other than too fast.

There are many articles available on the internet on rigging plastic rubber baits and eels too. Look them up if this is a technique that intrigues you. In particular I can recommend a few websites such as stripersonline.com, surfcasting-rhodeisland.com, longislandsurffishing.com, saltwateredge.com, striped-bass.com, surfrats.com and noreast.com. These are fantastic websites with many articles on surf fishing. In addition, their message boards feature lively discussions on many subjects from knots to plug colors twenty four hours a day.

Smaller versions of these slender baits, particularly the Fin-S and Cocahoe minnows are very effective early in the year when fish are feeding on smaller baits. Cocahoe minnows are usually the first lures I start the season with when I am looking for schoolie stripers on the warm mud flats of Long Island's north shore bays and harbors. They are also very effective during the summer run of weakfish which generally are smaller than their spawning siblings that dominate the surf scene in late May and early June.

There are other soft plastic baits that have become a mainstay in a surf caster's bag in recent years such as the paddle tail lures made by Storm and Tsunami. Their lifelike profiles and good casting properties make them very productive under a variety of conditions. Work them with a simple straight retrieve and the paddle tail will flutter and provide all the necessary action you need. Occasionally I find that adding a twitch to the retrieve works wonders especially when fish are hitting "short" or you feel many bumps but have few actual hook-ups. When employing this type of retrieve, the lure will momentarily flutter toward the bottom after the twitch, as the angler picks up the slack. Many times the fish will become more aggressive toward the perceived dying bait than they are towards one swimming straight. Here again I like the 3 or 4 inch models early in the spring while the 5 and particularly the 6 inch models are my favorite from late May till the end of the season.

These same manufacturers also produce a massive 9 inch model which some surfcasters have used to rack up impressive scores." Crazy" Alberto Knie who is one of the best known surfcasters in the Northeast, has landed 9 fish over 40 pounds in a recent season with 6 of those cows engulfing these large shads. Enough to put any reservation you might have about these large lures into a distant memory. They are an excellent choice for casting off of jetties with a conventional stick. Some of these lures weigh upwards of 6 ounces and very few spinning rods are able to carry that kind of a load. Conventional rods can usually carry heavier loads better. In addition, I feel the lure can be better controlled with conventional reels. I like to use these lures around rocks during periods of a waning current or just after the current turns. Big stripers will often

Large rubber shad have accounted for some big fish catches in recent years.

cruise around the base of the rocks, at this time, looking for small blackfish. Regardless of their length these lures are a great imitation of many bait fish in our water such as peanut bunker, shad, herring and even small blackfish. The only thing I don't like about these lures is that their hooks, while sharp, are also brittle and will bend or break. Therefore, when using these lures consider loosening your drag, especially if you fish with braid. Not doing so just might eventually contribute to you losing that fish of a lifetime!

CHAPTER SIXTEEN

— BOTTLE PLUGS —

There was a time, not too long ago, when bottle plugs were so effective on large bass and gorilla bluefish that few anglers dared to leave home without a few in their surf bags. For many they became primary weapons in their never-ending quest for big bass. Some remarkable catches were made on these lures, none more impressive that I am aware of, than the 64 lb striper landed under the fabled Montauk Lighthouse by Mark Malenovsky in November of 1992. If the sheer size of this monstrous fish wasn't surprising to some, the fact that he managed to land it in one of the most inhospitable places to fish on the east coast surely was. A yellow Gibbs 3 ounce bottle plug did the trick. To this day the yellow bottle plug is considered the "must have" color, not only because of Mark's catch but because it produced before and after his fish.

Bottle plugs or Casting Swimmers as they are also known have lost some luster in recent years primarily because of the type baitfish we have had in the surf lately. Because of their large profile, they are most effective when large baits like herring, shad and bunker are running in the surf. For many years, November could be counted to produce a steady supply of big bass on the eastern end of Long Island. Herring would make their return appearance in these waters after spending the summer months in the colder waters to the north. Sadly, this has not occurred with consistency lately but we keep our fingers crossed for future years.

Fishing is unpredictable in nature. Otherwise we would call it "catching" if we could just catch fish at will. It is hard trying to decipher why certain

With their large profiles bottle plugs are great imitations of herring, shad and bunker.

baits are present or missing from areas which generally are known to hold them. With this in mind, if you get some accurate information that a bite is happening on big bait get your behind out to the beach instantly. You can't count any more that the action will last for days, never mind weeks. I don't want to give you the idea that bottle plugs are only productive when big bait is around, not at all. They are very versatile lures that can be used under a variety of situations and locations. However, I want to stress the point of just how productive these lures are when gamefish are feeding heavily on larger size baitfish.

Bottle plugs are unique plugs which when properly retrieved create great tension on the rod and make it pulsate. Unlike darters and needlefish, which are retrieved under light tension, with the bottle plug, you'll always know when your plug is digging in the water. You will feel it in the rod! A steady retrieve is all that is necessary although during stormy conditions you might have to jerk the lure as soon as it lands in the water to "dig" it into the rough surf. Because of the tension that is created when the lure's scooped face is digging in the water, there is rarely ever a mistake made of not knowing when the strike occurs. The hits can be vicious especially when plugging with braided lines and graphite rods. There is very little room for error as the hooks can get pulled out if your drag is too tight. Bottle plugs are great plugs to use during stormy conditions because they can be punched through the wind and will dig into the rough surf when other lures are generally useless. When fishing open beaches during stormy conditions, I like to keep my bottle plug burrowed into the wave as long as possible. In addition I will take a few steps towards the ocean when the wave is receding so my plug doesn't pop out of the wave. I do have to warn you to be careful with this as big waves can sneak up on you very quickly. As you probably know by now, you can't outrun the darn things. The bigger the sets of water, the more useful bottle plugs become so keep this in your mind the next time you hear about a nor'easter barreling up the coast.

Under normal conditions I like to use big bottle plugs in the same places that I use darters, especially fat bodied ones that usually run deeper than slimmer models. Deep inlet rips or even shallower ones that feature fast water like the one under the Montauk lighthouse or a deep rip like at Shagwong Point can be great places to use big Gibbs bottle plugs. For places where the water is shallower, including all sandy beaches, I prefer the Super Strike Little Neck swimmer or the smaller Gibbs 2 ounce model. Work them by casting up tide; jerk them once to get them under the surface and retrieve only as fast as the water lets you. Usually a slow retrieve works best once the plug has dug in. This is enough to have this lure wiggle tantalizingly under the surface. Although these lures are primarily used in rough surf, I have used them religiously over the past few years in moderate conditions on sandy beaches with a lot of success. In fact, I rarely will head to the beach these days without one in my bag I employ the same strategy as when using metal lips in white water, casting them behind the wave and then digging them into the foam. Bottle plugs are also excellent lures when the fish are present but holding out of the reach of a metal lip swimmer. They are not known for their effica-

Super Strike and Gibbs Lures produce great bottle plugs, in a range of sizes and patterns.

199

cy in calm surf although it's hard to argue with the fact that they might be the best imitation of large bait. If that type of bait is present where you fish you might want to give them a try in calmer waters too. Use the smaller two ounce model from Super Strike and Gibbs and work them via sweeps of your rod and after picking up slack, sweep them again. The bottle plug will wobble when swept and flutter toward the surface while you are retrieving the slack in your line. You have to admit this does not make a bad presentation even though it is a bit unorthodox.

When it comes to colors, I suggest that you think of which baitfish is most prevalent in the surf at the time of your expedition and choose accordingly. I carry the following colors in my bag at all times: yellow over white, blue over white and all black. Not necessarily because they imitate any particular bait but because I have such a high degree of confidence in these patterns. I explained earlier why I think that confidence in a lure or a color is more important than the actual model or manufacturer and for me the best example of this is the bottle plug.

TIP

Bottle plugs don't lend themselves to being easily modified like many other plugs. All the angler can do is change a hook to a larger size and add a bucktail treble on the tail to slow down the wiggle of the plug. I don't like the hooks that come with Gibbs or Super Strike plugs and I would suggest you remove them immediately after purchase and replace them with similar size cut VMC Permasteel hooks.

CHAPTER SEVENTEEN

— TINS —

Tins are probably the most underutilized weapons a surfcaster has at his disposal. I can say this with a clear conscience because I know my habits and those of my friends and none of us use tins as much or as often as we should. This is primarily caused by the same reason why many lures find a warm corner of the bag and don't come out to play very often. The reason is lack of confidence. Most anglers use them when fish are out of range and they need a long cast to reach them or in heavy winds as tins are probably the only lure that will cut through the wind like a hot knife through butter. We also cast them into schools of breaking bluefish, not willing to feed good wood to their razor sharp teeth. When it comes to searching for fish however, most surfcasters will opt for a popping plug or a metal lip swimmer. If you think about it, in daytime most of the fish will remain close or on the bottom. They might be a foot off the sand or rubbing against it, the point is they will be where tins are usually retrieved. Why then toss a metal lip or popper? One of the mysteries of life, I guess.

I must admit I am always impressed when I see Ralph Votta, the fellow behind Charlie Graves Tins, working a tin for hours, usually with very impressive results as compared to those around him plugging with wood or plastic. It is not a mystery why these lures are so productive. Their long silvery shapes imitate many baitfish found in our waters, plus their sides flutter with silver flash as the sun's ray's reflect off them during a retrieve.

They are great imitators of many species in our water and they come in so many shapes and sizes that they basically can imitate any fish with a silvery side. Sand eels, spearing, butterfish, snappers, peanut bunker and bay anchovy are just some of the baitfish that tins closely resemble. Of course, the trick is to find out exactly what baitfish the game fish are feeding upon and then try to pick the right shape and size tin to match that forage. In addition, we must take into consideration at what depth the baitfish are swimming and what is their general preference in regards to habitat, in order to try to emulate this with our retrieve.

For example, sand eels are fond of burrowing themselves in the sand to escape the effects of strong currents and to hide from predatory gamefish. This behavior becomes the essence behind the approach for using a tin resembling a sand eel. The tin must be fished close to the bottom and occasionally dragged through the sand making intermittent "puffs" of sand to give the impression the sand eel is digging itself into the ocean bottom. Consider that stripers often just see this puff of sand and then react to strike the tin.

Another benefit of using a tin that closely matches the prevailing baitfish in the surf is what some like to call, the "schooling" effect. Many bait fish such as spearing, for example, like to travel in tightly packed schools, looking for safety in numbers. When using a tin, baitfish will often mistake it for one of their own and will follow the tin towards the shore creating a baitfish "schooling" effect. This benefits us in two ways. First, because of increased movement behind the tin, it creates a much more appealing target to the predatory fish who are not exactly enamored with the idea of chasing after a single baitfish up and down the beach. The second and equally desirable effect is that the baitfish that have been trailing the silvery tin will disperse sensing the threat from the gamefish hot on their tails. However your tin will remain in the strike zone, wobbling vulnerably. It becomes a focal point of the game fish's attention often resulting in a strike and a hookup.

Tins are primarily considered daytime lures because of the need for sunlight to emit the flash that attracts predators. But recently there has been some interest for their use at night especially since the sand eel population appears to be increasing and dragging a tin through the sand can be done either during the day or at night. Furthermore, some anglers and tin

Black tins like ones made by Point Jude are deadly in the dark, particularly when used with rubber trailers.

manufacturers are painting their tins various colors so that they can be seen at night by game fish. Some anglers have also taken the versatility of a tin step further and are using baking powder paint, the type used on bucktails, to change the color of their tins. Painting the tin a darker pattern on the top and lighter or plain white on the bottom is a very effective way to mimic the color pattern of most of the baitfish found in our area. Most baitfish and game fish for that matter have darker shaded backs and a lighter belly that helps them blend better into their surroundings and avoid predators. High visibility colors like yellow, chartreuse or parrot are very effective in daytime and particularly when water clarity leaves a lot to be desired. After a storm has passed through our area or when we receive excessive rainfall in a short period of time, bright colors like yellow or parrot can often be very effective in the dirty, muddy water. Their high visibility makes them an excellent choice under these conditions as fish can't hit what they can't see and these colors help our lure get noticed.

Tins are great casting lures and pack a lot of power in relation to their weight to size ratio. As a result they are very aerodynamic, can cut through the strongest winds and will generally outcast any lure under just about every condition. This makes them great candidates for use in stormy weather conditions when wind can make the presentation of wooden or plastic lures difficult and sometimes impossible. Given their excellent casting ability they also make a great delivery tool for a teaser. I like to attach my teaser to my swivel via a short piece of heavy mono leader. When rigged in this manner, it appears that the tin is chasing after a smaller bait fish. This will often draw an instinctive strike from a game fish that might hit the teaser out of sheer competitiveness or because it presents a larger sized meal. Either way it will be attached to your hook. Another benefit beyond the distance a tin reaches, is its single hook design which makes a quick release very easy, plus its ability to keep its original shape and shine regardless of how many times you hit a rock or how much time it spends in the jaws of bluefish.

As tins come in many sizes and shapes there really isn't one retrieve that will work for all styles. In addition, wind strength; current speed and white water will have an influence on how we retrieve each particular model. My advice would be to spend some time on a pier or a jetty so you can observe the tin on the retrieve and familiarize yourself with its movement and the speed it should be retrieved at in order to obtain the best possible action. Many of the tins have a wobbling or side-to-side action already built into them and a straight retrieve is the most effective one to use with this type of tin. On a sandy beach you can afford to go a little slower because the chance of getting snagged on a rock or weeds is nil to zero. In rocky areas however tins are generally not very good producers, as

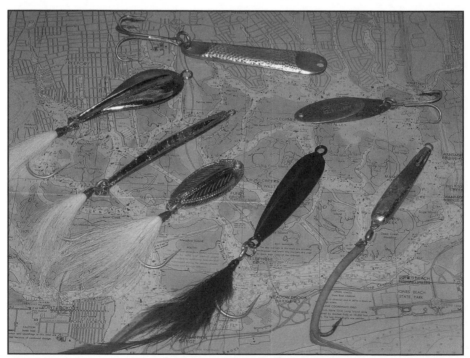

Elongated tins are a staple of Northeast surfcasters who rely on them heavily when fish are feeding on long, thin profile baitfish like spearing or sand eels. Wide body tins come into their own when larger baitfish like peanut bunker, herring or butterfish enter the surf zone.

they have to be retrieved too fast in order to keep them out of the rocks. However, here again the versatility of tins come to the fore as you can use keeled tins under these circumstances. The keel keeps the tin riding above the rocks and the retrieve can be slowed to attract predators.

The small tins made by Kastmaster, are probably the one lure by which today's surfcasters got exposed to fishing as children. They are absolutely a deadly spearing imitation and drive snappers crazy in the summer. In larger sizes, the Hopkins "Shorty" has been my favorite for many years along with the Point Jude Nautilus. Both of these weigh over 3 ounces and cast like bullets in a headwind. Better yet, they are proven fish catchers.

If you are attempting to imitate a sand eel you can use tins such as the Deadly Dick or the models made by Point Jude and Charlie Graves. Basically, this type of tin should be long and slender. Wider body tins are better imitators of larger baitfish found in our waters particularly in the fall months. Peanut bunker, butterfish and herring are just some of the species that can be very effectively emulated by using a wide profile tin. I try to carry tins in profiles that vary with the season. Thin and slender in the spring, short and wider in the late summer and only large and wide in the early fall months. Then I revert back to thin and skinny once the sand eels make an appearance towards the end of the season.

When it comes to choice of hooks or trailers, you don't necessarily need to go with the hook that comes in the package. Most manufacturers use either a single or treble hook dressed with bucktail hair and this works well most of the time. There are times when long feathered hooks will out produce the ones tied with short bucktail, particularly when long ,slender baitfish like needlefish or squid are in the area. Long feathers behind the tin make for a great imitation of squid tentacles but keep in mind that you will give up some distance in return for the longer profile. In addition, plastic tubes have been utilized very effectively and not just with tins but also with diamond jigs. In fact, the use of these tubes is one of the favorite techniques of charter boat captains on the east coast. Green or red tubes should be threaded along the long shank. Once they reach the bend in the hook a small slice should be made allowing the tube to extend about an inch or two past the bend. The end should then be cut diagonally to make it appear more lifelike while the other end of the tube is pulled over the swivel and up to the tin.

One of the most unusual ideas to come down the pipe lately is the new line of Point Jude tins called "Black Knights". These tins have a black vinyl finish and are designed for use at night. The idea is that they imitate an eel and their wobbling motion will be picked up by a striper's lateral lines. I haven't put nearly as much effort into this technique as I should but if they prove to be anything like their Wobble Heads, they will become a mainstay in my bag. Wobble heads can be used by attaching either a whole dead eel or a large plastic bait and I have done very well with these heads since they hit the market a few years ago. They are designed to provide all the action so all the angler has to do is to figure out the optimal speed of the retrieve in order to keep it off the bottom. I particularly like to use 7 or 9 inch Slug-go's or Fin-S rubber baits in conjunction with the Point Jude Wobble Head. Just impale the rubber bait onto the hook and cast it out, it's that simple. Wobble heads alone will provide all the necessary action and make a rubber bait snake look like an eel swimming through the water.

TIP

Some anglers like to shake their rod vigorously once the lure has landed in the water. They feel that the silvery flash and commotion will be picked up by the lateral lines of stripers and the sharp eyes of bluefish.

CHAPTER EIGHTEEN

— TEASERS —

Using a teaser in conjunction with a wooden or plastic lure is a very effective way to catch striped bass, bluefish and weakfish. Teasers can range from carefully tied creations which closely resemble certain species of baitfish to just a few bucktail hairs tied together on the shank of a hook. They are generally thought to be productive for two reasons. First, they resemble small baitfish which are often difficult to imitate with a small lure. Second, they often induce gamefish to strike at the plug or the teaser out of sheer aggressiveness and competitiveness for food. A gamefish that might ignore a lure cast in its direction will often hit the same lure when a teaser is added in front of it. It is thought that the gamefish perceives the lure to be another fish in pursuit of a smaller baitfish. They are most productive in calm water inside inlets, harbors and bays. They lose some of their efficacy in white water on oceanfront beaches.

There are downsides to using teasers and it has to do primarily with loss of distance during the cast. Teasers, particularly large ones, add a lot of air resistance during the cast and will reduce distance with even the best

Teasers account for their share of large bass each year.

asting lures. Another disadvantage of using teasers occurs when fish are actively feeding and the chance of a "double-header" greatly increases. If you think having a bluefish with a nasty attitude attached to your lure is a handful, just imagine having two of them on at the same time! If that is not bad enough, having two blues with razor sharp teeth each pulling in different direction almost always results in a parted line. You not only lose the fish but also the plug and the teaser! This is why when fish are active I always remove the teasers from my leader.

I find teasers most effective when used in conjunction with subsurface plastic swimmers, with Bombers, Rebels or Mambo minnows being my favorites. I never use teasers with surface lures and I would urge you not to either. I've seen anglers use teasers attached in front of their pencil poppers. However I find this to be more of a disservice to this great plug than an aid in catching fish. When working a pencil popper it's often hard to obtain a solid hook-up as fish will quite often miss the plug, which is constantly moving. Imagine how a teaser behaves when attached to a pencil popper. It slaps the water on either side of the pencil popper in a four foot arc. Unless the fish possesses an uncanny ability to judge where the teaser will slap the surface next, your chance of hooking up with it will be slim to none. Using a teaser in conjunction with popping plugs presents similar difficulties. Poppers move forward with a consistent rhythm and now you add two targets for the fish to try to follow. It is hard enough to fool a fish with a single moving target, never mind adding another one.

Some plugs like darters and bottle plugs we use in order to present a large baitfish "profile" and if you use a teaser with them you are risking a chance of smaller, more aggressive fish engulfing your teasers and losing the opportunity of getting that bigger fish you seek. I find tins particularly effective with teasers as they are one of the few lures that we can cast a long distance even when a teaser is used. Needlefish lures also fit in this category but again, I will only use them as a delivery method for a teaser instead of a primary fish catching tool. You should also consider that when presented with weedy conditions the use of a teaser is always a no-no, as it becomes another piece of hardware that will get fouled up by weed. I should know, I fish in some of the weediest conditions on Long Island. In fact, a lot of my friends refuse to fish with me because of the chance of us encountering weed in locations I prefer, is almost guaranteed. Believe it or

Weakfish although voracious predators often show preference for smaller lures. Using a teaser ahead of a swimming plug is a great way to induce them to strike at either the teaser or a lure.

not, I actually find these weed infested waters more productive when weed is present than when the water is weed-free. I often wonder if this is because gamefish or baitfish use the weed to disguise their presence.

By now you are probably getting the feeling that I am not a great fan of teasers and you are correct. I find they are truly a "niche" technique which will greatly add to your score but you will have to give up quality to quantity. Yes, there have been some very impressive stripers landed on teasers over the years but these are more the exception than the norm. Most of the fish you will catch on teasers will end up being of a smaller variety. Be that as it may, sometimes the only way to entice the fish to the hook will be via teasers. When fish are feeding on small bait or when most of the fish in the area are small, using teasers is the most productive strategy. We also need to take into consideration the type of species we are seeking to tangle with. I find that bass and bluefish will hit a lure of just about any size yet weakfish often show a fickle side and ignore larger lures. They will however rarely pass on a well placed teaser probably because most of their diet consists of small grass shrimp and other tiny baitfish.

Although we are technically able to attach thousands of trailers to a single hook and call it a "teaser" I generally prefer two types when searching for stripers or blues. A simple teaser made from bucktail hair or bucktail in conjunction with a few feathers is something I use most of the time. They are simple to tie, durable and I am able to present a different "look" to the gamefish by going with longer or shorter profiles. I also like Red Gill teasers as these elongated rubber baits are an excellent choice when fish are feeding on thin profile baitfish like sand eels. When I am targeting weakfish, in addition to bucktail teasers, I find DOA shrimp bodies very effective. Plastic worms, grubs and squid skirts, I find much more effective when used in conjunction with leadheads.

There are basically two ways to add a teaser in front of your lure. One involves adding a dropper loop about a foot and a half ahead of the lure and attaching a teaser directly to the loop. Rigged in this manner you don't need to be concerned with the teaser fouling up your leader during the cast or the retrieve. The other technique is to add the teaser via a short length of mono to the leader swivel. This is attached to the same end of the swivel to which the leader is also attached. When rigged in this manner the teaser can get tangled up around the leader. To avoid this, I like to use stiff leader material to attach the teaser to the swivel. This way the stiffness of the leader will at least, to some degree, keep the teaser away from the main line.

CHAPTER NINETEEN

— CONSERVATION —

We live in times during which fish populations are increasingly coming under pressure from both the recreational and commercial sectors. The number of humans on this planet of ours, is increasing every day and the oceans are looked upon by some nations as a never-ending supply of food or a convenient sewer. Research has however shown that many fisheries cannot support any more fishing pressure than they already receive. Armed with this knowledge we all must do our part to protect these species for future generations of fisherman. I think we can all agree that conservation ethics have had a profound effect on the way we look at gamefish. Today's surfcaster looks at these magnificent creatures more as a worthy adversary than tonight's dinner. I don't suggest that taking an occasional fish for the family dinner table is wrong, not at all. In fact, I think those who consume some of their catch become even more respectful of all the creatures Mother Nature provides to us. So as recreational anglers we must all play our part in helping to conserve and protect the fish we seek. Here are a few things we can all do very easily.

CRUSH YOUR BARBS

Before you ever set a hook on a fish you can do a few things to reduce the chance of injury to you and the fish and to increase the fish's survival chances after release. On the lures that feature three sets of trebles I like to remove the middle treble as long as it doesn't impair the action of the lure. Stripers must swallow their

In rocky areas it is safer for the fish and the angler to slide the fish onto the rock instead of holding it vertically.

meals head first because they lack defined teeth structure and can only crush their prey, therefore they generally will hit the front of the plug and consequently end up attached to the front hook. Bluefish on the other hand are notorious for their razor sharp teeth and their tendency to bite the tail of baitfish and chop them in half. For this reason bluefish will usually hit the back hook of a plug. With this in mind I remove trebles from the back of most of my plugs and I replace them with a single Siwash hook dressed sometimes with a little bucktail. In addition, I crush the barb to facilitate releasing bluefish which can be a handful particularly at night. I do not however like to crush the barbs on the front hooks. Some of my friends do and they swear that this does not result in many dropped fish as long as the angler keeps constant pressure on the fish so that the hook doesn't back out. For some reason I have a fear of losing that fish of my dreams if I crush the barbs on the front treble hook .The way I see it, I get in my own way just fine and my klutziness has cost me plenty of fish in the past.

Minimal handling during the unhooking process helps fish recover faster.

I don't need another thing to aggravate my occasional incompetence even further. On bucktails or similar single hook lures, I would advise against crushing barbs as chances of your losing the fish in my opinion are too high. I never was enamored with the idea of removing the back hook on the plug completely. I feel that on many plugs, particularly metal lips swimmers, removing the back hook alters considerably the action and the balance of the plug. In addition, the back hook, especially when dressed with a bucktail or a feather adds so much to the action of the plug that you might do yourself a real disservice by removing it. I can't tell you how many times I have seen an angler with a tail hook dressed with bucktail out-fish everyone around them.

You should also considerer carrying a hook dislodger tool. It comes in very handy when the hook is buried deep in the fish's mouth. These tools are inexpensive and take very little room on your belt or in your bag. All that is usually needed is to apply pressure downward on the hook with this tool and the hook should come free.

When it comes to the actual act of handling the fish a surfcaster should take his safety into account as much as the well being of the fish. Even the fish that looks spent can come to life at any moment and you should never let your guard down during the unhooking process. I've had many close calls over the years and that is part off the reason why these days I use a Boga Grip to assist me during the release. My dependency on this tool has made some of my friends actually make fun of me as I often refuse to handle the fish with my hands if it's not necessary. Instead, I take my time to get the jaws of the Boga Grip around the lips of the fish. If possible, I prefer to keep the fish in the water during the release process but I understand that this is sometimes difficult, especially when standing on jetties or rocks.

With stripers I always first try to get my Boga around the lips but if that is not possible I'll grab the fish by the jaw with a very firm grip. Once you commit yourself to doing this do not let your guard down or decrease the pressure as the hooks are usually inches from your hand. One shake of its head and you'll be in a world of trouble. If the striper is large I would advise against lifting the fish vertically from the water as the jaws might not support the weight of the big fish. There also will be gravitational pressure generated on its internal organs and this can do some major damage to the fish without you ever knowing it. A better way is to slide the fish onto the sand or onto a rock with care.

We should all try to minimize the handling of the fish as this removes the protective slime from their bodies. If you find that it is necessary to grab the fish, wet your hands before you touch it as this will limit the transfer of slime from the fish to your hands. Dragging a fish through the sand will also remove a fish's protective slime. Under all circumstances try to avoid contact with the gills of fish as they serve the same function as human lungs and you can do some major damage by sticking your fingers in there. Some anglers have gone to using gloves when fishing. Gloves make it easier to handle the fish and provide a bit of protection from hooks accidentally penetrating your skin.

Proper release has a lot to do with the ability of fish to recover quickly. Make sure that the fish has sufficiently recovered before releasing it into the water.

Weakfish and particularly bluefish always present a bit more of a challenge and I would strongly advise against putting your fingers in their mouths. Bluefish have very sharp rows of teeth while weakfish have four long teeth that are like the teeth in dogs. In fact, the name of the teeth, canines, comes from the fact that they are similar to the ones in dogs. Therefore, you do not want to get your hands anywhere in the vicinity of the razor sharp teeth of a bluefish or the puncturing canines of weakfish. These fish have earned the reputation as being the most difficult gamefish to control during the release process. If I can't get my Boga Grip around the lips of a bluefish, which actually is a common occurrence considering how much thrashing they do, I will try to grab the fish by the shoulders, just behind its gills and above its stomach. This usually quiets them down for a few moments. The grip should be firm but not strong enough to damage the fish.

After removing hooks from a fish it should be returned to the water as soon as possible. If the release process was quick all that is usually needed is a few moments of holding the fish horizontally in the water before it regains its strength. This process is necessary in order for the fish to regain oxygen from the water that passes over its gills. If the fish does not show eagerness or strength to go on its own a little help should be given by the angler by holding the fish lightly under the belly with one hand while the second hand should be placed just ahead of the tail. Holding the fish this way will enable you to move the fish back and forth in the water which will stimulate its ability to recover faster as it will hasten the absorption of oxygen and bring the fish back to life. A second technique that can be used to revive only striped bass, not blues or weakfish, because of their teeth, is to place your thumb in the mouth of the bass and gently drag the fish through the water so that water runs through its gills. With your thumb in its mouth this opens the mouth so that water can enter more freely. Larger fish usually require a bit more time to recover than smaller ones so take that into consideration when you are letting that big cow back into its habitat. You will know when the fish is ready to go as the dorsal fin becomes erect and its gills start to flare. At this point the fish will often start wiggling its tail, signaling to us that it's ready to go back on its own. This is the time to release the fish.

As to the subject of bluefish I want to mention that there are certain individuals in the fishing community who consider bluefish and most other fish without stripes a "trash" fish. You can easily identify these "sportsmen" by their behavior as they can often be observed kicking the fish back into the water as if it were a football or even worse throwing it on the beach in the direction of sea gulls. This kind of behavior must stop and each one of us should do our part to educate these ignorant fools of the importance of all the fish that are swimming in the ocean. Every species of fish plays an important part in the ecological food chain and they should all be returned to their habitat with care and unharmed.

THINK OF TOMORROW...

I think you'll agree that there are few things more satisfying in this sport than watching large stripers gracefully making their way through the surf. Doing your part in protecting this great resource will go along way in insuring that our kids will have the opportunity to join us in catching these magnificent creatures in future years. Just imagine the thought of your son or daughter catching a fish of a lifetime and the possibility that it all happened because you released this same fish with care many years ago. It is enough to motivate me to take the few extra moments and safely release all of my fish. Like it or not, we have been entrusted with protecting these species for future generations and we must rise to the challenge. I understand that there are many factors that are out of our control from pollution to loss of habitat but we must strive to do more to protect and save these fish. Too many among us still feel it's acceptable to kick a fish back into the surf. It is our duty as the "keepers of the beach" to educate those around us about the importance of conservation and releasing fish unharmed. If we do not do it, I ask you, who will?

CHAPTER TWENTY

— TAKE A KID FISHING —

We are living in an age of instant gratification. No generation before us has ever put such a high emphasis on satisfying personal desires than the current one. We are becoming so enamored with ourselves and our personal accomplishments that the things I consider most important in life, our families, are taking a back seat to personal goals. Our kids are bombarded with toys from video games to a myriad of television channels tailored to their needs, all designed to keep them chained to the couch each day as long as possible.

Watching your kid fight a fish will create memories that you both will cherish for a long time.

I often reminisce about my childhood days in Croatia if for no other reason other than them being the days before life got so complicated. We had a single television channel which worked only part of the day and even then it was filled with communist propaganda and hard news. Not much for a kid to get interested in, that's for sure. So we spent days playing pretend cowboys and Indians in the forest around our home, playing soccer barefoot in the open fields or just swimming in the crystal clear Adriatic Sea from morning to dusk. But most of all we fished. I lived on a small island in a village which had a population of a less than 200 people. Our house which was hand built by my grandfather and his brothers was a stones throw away from the water and every morning we awoke to the smell of sea salt in the air and the calls of hungry sea gulls. After school each day, I would grab a piece of stale bread and soak it in the seawater. Then I would form little dough balls which I used for bait. Once in awhile my grandmother would bring home some sardines from the "Pescaria" (a local seafood market) and I would mix the juice from the can with the bread as a little added attractor. As I got older and girls became "the" focal point of the lives of my friends, I continued fishing, often at night. All the while, I had to endure the scorn of my friends because I usually preferred fishing to partying.

My parents divorced when I was young, each going their own way and entrusting my grandparents with my care. In a way I was lucky because I don't think I could have ever received more love and attention than I did. My grandparents struggled to provide me with some sense of normalcy in

Snappers are a great way to introduce kids to fishing.

the days when a divorce still had a lot of stigma attached to it, especially in a small village. Fishing gave me an outlet to express myself and to find some peace alone with my thoughts. I also had a strong desire to follow in my grandfather's footsteps who I consider to this day one of the best fishermen of his generation. No one could match his prowess for finding fish or shoals in the middle of nowhere by only using landmarks and intuition. I don't know if I will ever succeed in even coming close to his legacy but Grandpa, if you are reading this, thanks for everything.

As I became a parent of two wonderful children I wanted to pass onto them my love of fishing. My son Steven enjoys casting in the surf as much as our boat trips, while Michelle, my little princess, particularly enjoys our party boat family trips. One summer after a long day on the construction site, I needed to cool off and clear my head. I grabbed my son who at the time was about eight years old and we headed off towards Jones Inlet on Long Island to do some sunset casting. As much as I wanted to get out of the house, I wanted even more to peel him off the video game controls. I picked the spot in the inlet where we would be protected from the waves but to get to it we had to scale down many large boulders. I carried him and all our gear over the boulders and upon reaching my chosen destination lowered him on a big, flat rock and told him not to move from there. I fished with my trusted St.Croix Tidemaster six foot rod while he had a rod that he had just received as a birthday gift a few days before. It was one of those "spaghetti" rod and reel combos that bends like a pretzel and was spooled with what looked like six pound test monofilament. I rigged a three inch Storm by tying directly to the thin monofilament. I wasn't really expecting to catch fish; practice casting was more what I had in mind. Besides, I thought a single hook lure would be a lot safer than a bunch of trebles hanging around his ear. We fished a small rip on the inside of the inlet and his casts were oh, about 15 yards long, if that much. After a few casts he declared he was "stuck" for the umpteenth time. As I reached over to try getting him unstuck his line went limp and he reeled in half a Storm lure with the paddle tail cleanly cut off. I tried to explain to him that a bluefish had chopped his lure in half but this was falling on deaf ears. He insisted he was stuck and that a crab probably cut the lure with its claws. Exasperated, I gave up trying to explain to him that he just received his first hit in the surf. I guess for us parents, these things hold much larger significance than they do for our children as my son was totally unfazed by what had happened.

I wish I could remember when my first hit occurred when I was child, but I was delighted to be present to witness my son's first one. I attached another Storm to his line and he was back casting, apparently oblivious to the significance this moment held. Suddenly his rod started to bend like a wet noodle with the tip almost touching the reel. I watched in shock as the thin monofilament peeled off his reel while he kept reeling against the drag. I leaned my rod on some rocks and watched him with a look of glee and horror on my face. Witnessing your child hook his first fish was a remarkable experience filling me with pride and joy but knowing that the thin mono was going to part as soon as it came in contact with some barnacle covered rocks was tough to swallow. Remarkably, the fish changed direction and took off with the tide toward the bay. Still, I knew that our chance of actually landing this fish among the boulders at the base of the jetty was slim but darn if I was going to tell him that. While he followed my directions intently I hopped onto the bolder closest to the water's edge, hoping to maybe get a shot at the fish before it started thrashing at the base of the jetty.

Because this was one of his first trips to the surf, I never bothered to use a leader. All I was planning was to give him an opportunity to practice his casting but now I was stuck in a predicament that would likely result in heartbreak. As I caught the first glimpse of the fish cruising close to the surface, I was in for another surprise. Golden sides flashing in the late day sun made me do a double take but even then the scene in front of us remained the same. A weakfish in excess of seven pounds was cruising along, disappearing into the rip again and peeling line. My heart started to beat even faster as these fish were hard to find in those years.

Steven Hromin with a "lost" weakfish.

My son Steven managed to regain most of the line and the fish was but three yards away from the rock I where I was standing. I knew that I only had one shot, one chance to try to get my Boga Grip around its jaw. Touching the 6 pound test monofilament would have definitely resulted in a parted line. The same fate was in store for us should the line come in contact with the rock. I also knew from experience that the fish would start to thrash around as soon as it sensed the rocks. If I failed to slip my Boga around its jaws on the fist try, the end result would be the same, a parted line. I said a quiet prayer and lunged at the fish which almost instantaneously started to beat the water into a froth with its tail. In horror I felt my Boga slip out of my hand and disappear into the water. The surface got strangely quiet as the foam started to dissipate while my son stood on his rock oblivious to what just happened. His mono was curled around the tip of his rod, broken under the strain of the thrashing fish. Embarrassed and defeated I reached for my lanyard to which my Boga was attached and started to retrieve it from the water when I got the surprise of my life. The weakfish was attached to the Boga!!! When my son saw me lift the fish out of the water his eyes widen up with pride and amazement.

I have landed some nice fish over the years including some that were a pound or two shy of that magic 50 pound mark. But no fish brought me more joy than that golden beauty. There is something special about a father standing next to his child while he is beaming with pride, witnessing and sharing the moment together. To boot, I became a hero that day for miraculously pulling the "lost" fish out of the ocean. At that minute I knew that my life as a fisherman will never be defined by the size or amount of fish I catch. Instead it will be defined by my children remembering the times we spent together fishing. Fishing trips on party boats and in the surf, little league games or just a little basketball in the driveway, these are the things I want to be remembered for. If I don't catch another fish in my life I could live contently with memories of watching my kids doing what made them happy.

Take your own kids fishing and create your own special memories. I can guarantee that years from now, when the kids are all grown up and you sit in front of the fireplace on a cold winter's night, memories of those trips will warm your heart. Remember, the most memorable life is one spent making memories, so take your kids fishing!

— ABOUT THE AUTHOR —

Zeno Hromin is a veteran surfcaster whose love of the surf had humble beginnings. From his days as a child hand lining off the coast of Croatia, in the Adriatic Sea, to traveling the east coast today looking to tangle with big feisty stripers, Zeno has shared his experiences on the internet and in print. He has written for many fishing websites as well as for The Fisherman and On the Water magazines. As a member of the High Hill Striper Club, one of the oldest surf fishing clubs in New York, Zeno has won numerous awards in club competition and in competing in the New York Surf Fishing Contest. He is very conservation minded and releases almost all of his fish each season. Recently, he became a recipient of the 2007 Grampa Old Spook Memorial Award in recognition of his willingness to help others and also for his involvement in fundraising for the Send-A-Kid Fishing Program. Zeno is a member of the New York State Outdoor Writers Association and he resides with his family in Westbury, New York.

— NOTES —

— NOTES —